GOLEM:
LEGENDS OF THE
GHETTO OF PRAGUE

A "Golem" is an artificial man made by qabalistic magic
and legends of this strange being extend back at least to
the ghettos of medieval Germany. The Golem was created
to serve its creator.

Chayim Bloch

ISBN 0-7661-0111-8

To the Memory of the great Master and Champion
of the Jewish Cause

DR. JOSEPH S. BLOCH

former Rabbi and Member of the Austrian Parliament

(born 30. Nov. 1850, died 1 Okt. 1923)

Monument to Rabbi Judah Loew

Wagner (anxiously):

Welcome! to the Star of hours.
(low)
But let not word or breath escape you
A glorious work will be completed now.

Mephistopheles (lower):

What is it then?

Wagner (lower):

A man is in the making.

Goethe, "Faust", IInd part, 2nd act.

CONTENTS

I spent the winter 1923—1924 in New York. I found a loving reception there in the intellectual Jewish Circle and gained many true friends whom I made mention of in grateful remembrance in my description entitled, "With our brothers in New-York".*

To the Editor of the Jewish Tribune, the most important Jewish Weekly Magazine in America, Mr. Hermann Bernstein, I owe the acquaintance of Mr. Harry Schneiderman, Secretary of the American Jewish Commitees and Editor of the American Jewish Year Book. With deep emotion I here offer him my thanks for the full measure of brotherly love which he bestowed on me. He also procured me a splendid translation of this

---

* The description appeared in a series of articles in the Vienna Weekly Magazine for the Interests of Jewry "Die Wahrheit". It is being prepared in book-form.

book, parts of which he had printed in the Jewish Tribune.*

* * *

For centuries the legend that the Golem was still kept in the loft of the Old-New Synagogue had been current and many delightful tales, some of them humourous ones, are connected with it. This enticed a well-known writer, Egon Erwin Kisch, a son of Prague, to the bold, I might almost say hazardous undertaking of ascending into the loft of the Synagogue, in order to look for the "corpse" of the Golem. In a fine piece of word-painting, "On the track of the Golem" he gives us the description of his quest.** His trouble was in vain! He did not find the Golem. Then he pursued another clue, supplied by a further legend which he heard of during the war, to the effect that the servant of the exalted Rabbi Loew had carried off the Golem secretly from the loft of the Synagogue and had buried him on the Galgenberg, outside the town. (See the Chapter "Where lie the remains

---

* Those stories marked in the Index with * were translated by an English lady, Mrs. Loneck-Winterbotham.

** Egon Erwin Kisch, Der rasende Reporter, Berlin 1925, Erich Reiß-Verlag.

of the Golem?") Kisch thought it extraordinary how the dates of time and place agree with the historical reality. There was really a servant at the Pinkas Synagogue, Abrahm ben Secharja by name, and his grave stone is still to be seen in the old Jewish Cemetery. It is recorded on it that he died in the year 1602 and had held the office of templeservant for thirty years; that is in the time from which the legend dates. The statements referring to the way from the Pinkas Synagogue to the Zeiklergasse, correspond exactly with the oldest existing plans of the town. Kisch gives a detailed description of the Galgenberg where, according to the above-mentioned legend, the Golem found his last resting-place. He finishes his description with the words; "Standing by his grave, I know why God so willed it, that the Man-automaton, working ever for the wellfare of stangers and unconditionally subject to an extraneous will, should be irrecoverably buried here."

* * *

The stories of the Golem, appearing here, I originally printed in the year 1917 in the "Oesterreichischen Wochenschrift" edited by my Friend and Master Dr. Joseph S. Bloch. The late Chief-Rabbi of Vienna, Dr. Moritz Guedemann, wrote to me on this occasion: "... I believe your work to be a most valuable one, because your legends will be very fitted for the enlightenment of those non-Jewish circles who still believe in the use of blood by the Jews. It would be well to edit the collection in book-form."

The Chief-Rabbi of Jugo-Slavien, Dr. Isaac Alcalay in Belgrad, wrote in a letter addressed to me: "I had great pleasure in reading the legends about Rabbi Loew, in which fiction and truth are so beautifully interwoven. One feels a kind of rapture in reading these stories. I think that the same longing for deliverance, which led our ancestors to the compiling of such beautiful tales, also transports us into a beautiful dream, makes us forget the terrible truth and thus we feel so happy in the reading of such tales!"

CHAYIM BLOCH

AN INTERPRETER OF THE EAST TO THE WEST

*THE STORY OF CHAYIM BLOCH,
WHO HAS CREATED A SENSATION IN
LITERARY EUROPA*

BY

HARRY SCHNEIDERMAN

IN 1919, the literary circles of Germany and
Austria were treated to something so delight-
fully novel, so entrancingly new and yet de-
liciously reminiscent of centuries ago, that the
author of the new book at once became a bright
star on the sky of letters. The writer was a
Galician Jew, and his contribution was not in the
field of non-Jewish belles-lettres in which so
many Jews in all countries excel. The book which
he published and which was so enthusiastically
hailed by numerous critics and reviewers, was on
a purely Jewish subject, the value of which lay
in its success in interpreting to the Western world
the soul of the East European Jew. And this

success did not result from the author's ability as a sociological writer. He has no such ability. But he has a great and beautiful talent, and that is to tell a story. It was through the medium of a story, or rather, of a series of stories, that this man, in a few little volumes has done more to give the Western world an insight into that "mysterious realm," the heart of those Polish Jews who appear to prefer to live in their ghettos in a manner which has changed very little, if at all, during the past two hundred years, than many learned dissertations could have done.

This interpreter, this unconsciously skilfull teller of tales, is Chayim Bloch, who has just come to America where he will seek to secure funds for the publication of a monumental work which will make accessible a rich storehouse of source material of the history of the Jewries of Europe from the seventh century on.

It was during the World War that Bloch became notable as a writer. Before that he had lived the quiet existence of a well-to-do business man in Delatyn, Galicia, where practical affairs absorbed but little of his time and he was able to pursue those beloved studies which he had

14

begun in a Yeshibah. He was not interested in secular or "Western" learning, his studies at the seminary having been the sum total of his education. He soon developed a special love for delving into the legendary and mystical writing of his sect, the Chassidim, and occasionally he would write a little note on the history or the traditions of his group for the famous *Wochenschrift,* founded by the late Dr. Joseph S. Bloch, a namesake but not a relative. This peaceful life was rudely interrupted by the outbreak of the World War. In 1914, Bloch was thirty-three, married, and father of several children. He was slight, almost anemic, with weak, near-sighted eyes. The first soldiers sent to the front were the flower of Austria's manhood. Bloch, who had been disqualified from serving in the army in his youth, was naturally not invited to go to war. But something just as bad had happened to him and to all the Jews of the Eastern borderland—the Russian invasion. The Austrian Government was solicitous for the well being of its subjects in this region and, assuming that the Jewish population would be shown no mercy by the Muscovite hordes, ordered the removal of the Jews to the interior, and Bloch along with tens of thousands of others suddenly found themselves in Vienna, an outpost of Western civilization.

It was largely in order to secure a livelihood that Bloch began to contribute more voluminously to the *Wochenschrift*, which he was encouraged to do by the publisher and editor. As he found that the Eastern Jew, especially the Chassidim, were so little understood in the West, and that scarcely anything was known of their quaint legends about wonder-working Jewish saints, their sparkling humor and biting wit, it was natural that Bloch should turn to disclosing these riches to the eyes of the Occident.

But in 1915, Austria found that what the war required was not so much fighters as cannon-folder, and for this Chayim Bloch was just as suitable as any able-bodied man. So, we find him conscripted and wearing the Austrian uniform. He was even sent to the trenches where he stayed for nine months, during which he continued to write for the Vienna Jewish press. But he eventually succumbed to sickness; spent much time in a field hospital from which he was discharged, and, being certified as totally unfit for active service, was assigned to duty at a camp for war prisoners at Csót, in Hungary. Here he had leisure to pursue his literary work and, what is more, he met Jews from various parts of the word, from whom he learned their local legends and myths. Bloch's position at this camp was beautifully described in a recent issue of *Neues Wiener Journal* by the famous writer, Dr. Sándor Várhely, who tells how he came to know Bloch.

"It was in May, 1916," wrote Dr. Várhely, "I had left the Reserve Hospital at Sopron, where I had been confined for several months as a result of a wound suffered in the field, and because I was, on account of my lame foot, 'fit for garrison duty only', was ordered to a war-prison camp in the Veszpremer Department. At that time, the camp already had many thousands of captives—men (now it may be told) from all parts of Russia, Roumania, and Italy—and among them were several thousand Jews.

"Late in the evening, I arrived there in an automobile from Győr. Silently lay the foreign city, equipped with all comforts and modern fixtures, in the heart of the Bakony Forest. Every once in a while the cry 'Vigyáz!' (attention!)

would ring out, passing around the entire camp and awakening loud echoes in the forest. One of the soldiers belonging to the guard at the gate led me to the watch-tower, where I had to report to the officer on duty. I recognized in him a dear comrade in the field who, thanks to a fate similar to mine, was in this camp, far removed from barbed-wire entanglements and trenches, away from the din of cannonading. As it was magnificent outdoors, I decided, while it was still night, to make the rounds of the camp and inspect my new post of duty. My friend who was relieved just at this hour, was my guide. Between the hundreds of barracks blew a cool breeze and about the crescent moon little stars glittered; they looked down pityingly at the culture-world with its dumdum bullets.

"In front of the window of one of the shacks we came to a halt. We heard a deep, woful sobbing. In the dim light of a candle, a man was seated on the floor, bending low over a book and weeping. The melody was heartrending.

"My comrade, a non-Jew, was deeply moved, and said: 'That is a Jewish rabbi who, through the stupidity of the military authorities, was made into a soldier. He is now saying his prayers. This is his custom at this hour, night after night.' He did not know the man's name but he was able to describe to me how the man, even in the strait-jacket of military service, strictly observed all the ritual prescriptions, how he fasted when he could not get Kosher food, how he had wept before the camp commander to be excused from writing on the Sabbath, to which, incidentally, the latter, a splendid chap in every way, agreed. I at once thought the man must be a Chassid. having seen among the Chassidim many such deeply earnest faces.

"We could not resist going into the room. Softly, timidly, we entered. I had the feeling that I had stepped into a sanctuary. Bowed over a little book, in reverent ecstasy, he received us with a whisper and a sigh, all confused by our appearance—for it should be said that while Bloch is a good man, an expert Kabbalist, a man thoroughly versed in Jewish literature, as a soldier he was a terrible *Schlemihl*. He had not even mastered the art of saluting.

"I asked him whether things were going so badly with him in the army that he had to weep.

He replied: 'I must not lament over the fate which Heaven has sent to me. Besides, the Commandant as well as my other superiors have extended many courtesies to me; they have even assigned me a separate room, so that I may pursue my studies when off duty. My weeping, therefore, has nothing to do with my military service, but my nocturnal lamentations are over the destruction of our Temple, and only the Psalms which I was reading mowed me to tears."

"At this answer my eyes filled with tears. But I played the role of Joseph toward his brothers, I did not make myself known to him. To my further question, whether Jewish law was so unreasonable as to forbid the eating of *trefa* food even in war when *kosher* comestibles were not at hand, Bloch stood erect like a true soldier and answered: 'Discipline, Lieutenant! Discipline!' But a fire glittered in his eyes. He explained his reply in this fashion: 'According to the rules laid down by our sages, one may, in any emergency, also eat *trefa*, but I am attending school here. I am learning to keep discipline; therefore I would rather fast than eat *trefa,* because I have not the right to decide how great the emergency must be to release me from the prohibition against eating *trefa*.' I there upon, made myself known to him as a Jew, and became, from that day on, his friend and admirer.

"Sometime after this I had occasion to pass through another barracks in which Bloch had been ordered to make his new 'domicile'. It was late in the evening and the room was brightly lighted. Bloch was sitting at an ink-stained table and was working.

"Every once in a while he raised his left hand to his mouth and nibbled at a piece of stale bread, while with the right hand he wrote. I happened to come when he was working on his diary. This was entitled 'The War Diary of a Jew,' and on the first page was a poem, which impressed me so at the time that I copied it in my note book. It ran:

October 15
(About to leave for the front)

I

I am not the same as I was;
  Then, I knew only praying
And now I stand at hell's door,—
  They wish to send me to kill human beings.

II

I know not if mine is the guilt;
  Must my hands with blood be stained?
Must my mind on murder be bent?
  For this, God, did'st thou give strength to my
                                    limbs?

III

O God, is it Thy decree?
  Then do I Thy will without murmur;
Yet forgive a heart full of repentance
  And I go to my death unafraid!

"The diary contained unusually splendid reflections on humanity and Judaism. His words were prophecies—I see them now as realities!—and cries of protest against the Godlessness of Europe. I ordered him to destroy the diary at once; if it had fallen into the hands of a war-enthusiast, Bloch would have been haled before a court-martial and accused of being an agitator, a traitor, and God knows what else.

"Bloch told me again and again that he had faith in the goodness of Divine Providence, and that all these things which we have lived through are only the birth-pangs of a new humanity. I,

22

the witness of his hunger and his suffering, his deeds and his works, wish from the bottom of my heart that he may live to see the birth of this new humanity!"

While in the trenches Bloch wrote the book which made him famous. This was *"Der Prager Golem,"* the simple stories evolved by the child-like imagination of oppressed Jews of the medieval ghetto, about the wonder-work of their holy rabbis who, in times of danger, saved the Jewish community through the instrumentality of a Golem, a clay mannikin, miraculously endowed with life through formulas contained in the Kabbalah and other books of Jewish mysticism. This work was received with acclaim upon its publication in book form in 1919, and it was soon followed by *"Israel, der Gotteskämpfer,"* the story of the Golem made by Rabbi Elijah Baalschem of Chelm, and *"Die Gemeinde der Chassidim,"* a history of the origin, the teachings, and the traditions of Chassidim.

Bloch saw also that the West had an avid literary appetite for the proverbs, the aphorisms, and the humorous quips of the Eastern Jews, and he set himself to collecting and rendering these into German. Thus far, he has published two volumes in this field *"Ost-Jüdischer Humor"* and *"Hersch Ostropoler,"* the latter being accounts of the "monkey-shines" of a famous wag, Hirsch, a Jew of Ostropol. Bloch has also completed the manuscript of a collection of legends contained in the Kabbalah, but the financial upheaval in Central Europe has called a halt in the publishing of books for the time being.

The distinguished author is now in this country where he is seeking to interest patrons of Jewish learning in an extremely important work which he has partially completed. This will be called *"Ozar Chayim,"* a chronicle of life—the life of the Jews of Europe as reflected in the response the published answers of Rabbis to ritual questions put to them by members of the communities. These responses have been published since about the seventh century. Bloch has selected those which bear upon Jewish history, has arranged them according to topics, and has provided them with useful notes, critical remarks, and indices.

PREFATORY NOTE

HAVING been entrusted with the writing of a preface to Chayim Bloch's book of legends "The Golem of Prague", I address myself to this task with pleasure, all the more so as I have been busied for the space of almost four years with the problem of the Golem and that this book has supplied me with much valuable information. When I first caught a glimpse into this world of legends I was pleased with the richness of description in them, giving a flawless picture of this most mysterious legendary figure.

What I, in toilsome work, had slowly pieced together out the tenacious mass of material, I found confirmed here in the numerous documents, hidden until now from Westeuropean literature, of the late medieval Polish Judaism. The most important Jewish circle of culture after the zenith of Judaism in Germany had been passed.

25

But when we regard all these legends with respect to the problem of the Golem, the question as to the nature of this miraculous figure is, unfortunately, no more answered than it was before; and we only gain numerous facts from them, on which we can build up our inferences towards the solution of this significant question; as I have already done in my sketsch „Of the Golem and the Schem".*

It was not Chayim Bloch's work to define his position towards the Golem. Rather it was his task to collect the oldest of he legends circling round Rabbi Loew, a work which, as it seems to me, he has succeeded in marvellously well. It was possible for him to use the earliest legends connected with the question, which is all more important than the oldest German document dates only from the year 1808, in which year Jacob Grimm wrote the following words about the Golem in the "Zeitung für Einsiedler" (Paper for Solitaries):

"The Polish Jews, after having spoken certain prayers and observed certain Feastdays, make the figure of a man out of clay or lime which, after they have pronounced the wonderworking

---

* Allgemeine Verlagsanstalt, Munich.

Shem-ha-mphorasch over it, comes to life. It is true this figure cannot speak, but it can understand what one says and commands it to do to a certain extent. They call it Golem and use it as a servant to do all sorts of house-work; he may never go out alone. On his forehead the word *Aemaeth* (Truth; God) is written, but he increases from day to day and can easily become larger and stronger than his house-comrades, however small he may have been in the beginning. Being then afraid of him, they rub out the first letters so that nothing remains but *Maeth,* (he is dead) whereupon he sinks together and becomes clay again. But once the owner of a Golem allowed him to grow so tall that he could not reach his forehead. Then in his fear he told this servant of his to draw off his boots, thinking that in so doing he would stoop and that then he could reach his forehead. It happened as he thought it would, and the first letter was successfully erased, but the whole load of clay fell on the Jew and crushed him to death."

Grimm could say but little, compared to the importance which time has given to this question. Verbal tales and suggestions have worked together at the enlargement of our circle of legends up to

Meyrink's novel "The Golem", the wonderful success of which has brought the shadow-form of the Golem into everyone's notice. But the question of the nature of the Golem had always remained alive among some few adepts, as the possibility of the existence of such a being apparently lies in the consciousness of the people, though no-one knew the channels which could lead to the opening-up of the dark passages from where one hoped for the solution of the mystery. A deep and tragic desire of mankind, the possibility of the creation of artificial beings, was dragged into the open light of day—and the possibility of such creation as often passionately asserted or frantically refuted, as the impossibility of everything miraculous was claimed.

If, till then, little was known of the actual Creation of the Golem, so does Bloch's collection, especially in the legends "The Making of the Golem" and "The Golem is destroyed" as well as in the following comments, contain so much that is new and explanatory, that we at least find ourselves as much nearer to the cabbalistic mystery of the Golem as we can undoubtingly gather from the documents the exclusively cabbalistic prescription of this creation — a spiritual therefore in place of the magical, from which, according to popular imagination, the Golem had sprung. This is not the place to point out the value of this difference; may the establishing of the exclusively mystical basis to the creation of the Golem suffice; a subject which I have treated more nearly in my sketch on the Golem.

I have already mentioned that, by the help of this collection of legends, I have succeeded in putting my conclusions with regard to the Golem into a more convincing form. This fact is, I believe, to be welcomed all the more because the problem of the Golem does not only represent a Jewish question but, above all, a universal popular one which, like so many other universal human questions, has found it's best solution in Judaism.

There is hardly any object in trying to read anything of secret mystery into these legends; they come before us as the simple description of conditions which, from the figure of the Golem, have become the times of our forefathers. They appear before us without pretensions, as simple and modest witnesses of a mystery which, like the Messianic, is the hope of the believing Jew. They appear to me to be not only documents of any more or less significant human story. They are still alive in the strength of their belief, and the pulsing blood in them is ready still today to sacrifice itself for the distress and sorrow of it's unhappy people.

That is the life-giving and sacred nature of the legend, that she describes conditions which never dry up into history, as, full of living streams, she can call her heroes to life at any moment in order to prove their reality, by their life. So far as this goes the holy Rabbi never died—and the figure of the Golem only sleeps in the grave meanwhile, till Rabbi Loew, supplied with sacred life and the wisdom of the Book of *Jezirah* comes again to us and wakes his Golem from his deep sleep by the Thrice Holy Name, Enough of misery and sorrow is heaped on our poor world; it were the question of the deliverance of all by the secret of old Adam. *"Mizad ze ruach chayim":* for from this quarter does the spirit of Life flow.

Hans Ludwig Held.

30

INTRODUCTION

OF the many Jewish myths and legends
which have been immortalized by poets,
painters and prose-writers, and which are
eagerly welcomed by literateurs of today, the
tales about the Golem are undeniable the most
beautiful. No other Jewish myth possesses more
archaic charm, none has more power so deeply
to move the reader.

Before me lies a manuscript in the Hebrew
language and script, which bears the title "Nifloet
Mhrl," (The Miracles of Rabbi Loew). Redacted
about three hundred years ago, it is rich in tragic
episodes and enchanting tales. A narcotic fragrance suspires from these wonderful stories. They
tell of sorrows, of struggles, of triumphs.

The locality of these legends is Prague, the seat
of that ancient, venerable Jewish community;
that home of sages, scholars, saints and mystics;

the scene of a thousand wonders, innumerable horrors; that Prague at the hands of whose skillful masters there arose a city, the beauty and the quaintness of which have been left untouched down to our own day.

The fame of one name resounds in it—the name of Rabbi Loew, one of the greatest pillars of the *Goluth*, about whom tradition has wreathed a luxuriant garland of legends and woven a colorful tapestry of myths; but whose actual biography has remained a closed book even to the wide circle of scholars.

This legendary, radiant figure still shines upon the Jewish people with all the warmth, all the goodness, all the beauty and loyalty with which Rabbi Loew untiringly protected his harried co-religionists through almost an entire century (1513-1609). This man, to whom the people, out of gratitude and veneration, gave the title "Hohe," exalted, was of a divinely gifted nature. He had a heart overflowing with love, a soul which thirsted after righteousness, a character which throbbed in harmony with the threefold basic chord of ancient Jewish morality—modesty, compassion and kindness.

32

A contemporary of Rabbi Loew here tells, in unostentatious words and with impressive naiveté of the birth and the youthful years of this exalted personage, of his disputations with the Catholic eccleciastics of Prague, of the events which led him to fashion the Golem, and of all the deeds of wonder which he performed through this instrumentality.

Rabbi Loew was counselled "from Heaven" to make the Golem. By means of mystical formulas which were communicated to him in dreams, and whose structure and order it was his mission, as one of the most consummate expert Kabbalists to divine—although to decipher their secret meaning was doubtless no easy task for even his exalted spirit—he succeeded in giving life to the Golem. He shaped it of clay, endowed it with spiritual breath, and made it a doer of wonders.

Here, pure love of humanity justified the creation of the dreadful. and sanctified the terrible. And even out of this unadorned recital which I, substantially retaining the naiveté and the childishly awkward presentation of the unknown compiler, transmit to the reader, there is wafted to us the fragrant air of those olden times, of the power and the magic of the great personality of Rabbi Loew. How wholly beautiful and alluring, however, would these legends become were one of our poets to present them artistically!

In his famous novel "Der Golem," Gustav Meyrink says: "I really do not know what the origin of the Golem legend is, but that somewhere, something which cannot die haunts this quarter of the city and is somehow connected with the legend, of that I am sure."

Meyrink, to some extent, is right. This is to be clearly discerned also in these memoirs. Men who live amidst mysticism are at pains to prove that the exalted Rabbi Loew and all those saints and sages, before and after him, to whom is attributed the creation of a Golem, understood, thanks to their profound knowledge of the Kabbala, how to employ the *Shem ha-me forasch*, the preeminent name of God, so as to endow with life a shape formed by them. Those, however, who do not believe in and deny any justification for the mystical and the occult, aver that we have here to deal with a symbol, the allegorical meaning of which was eventually forgotten, because of the clearness and vividness of the symbol itself, which has consequently come down through the centuries with a sort of independent life of its own in the shape of a legend.

The Golem was formed of clay. It served its master dutifully and loyally; ultimately, however, it became mad and a danger to the entire city, so that its master had to turn it back again into earth, which he did by taking away from it the *Shem*, the sacred word, the life-principle. But all this notwithstanding, the Golem is not yet dead! It did not become a mere handful of dust which is cast to the winds or is thrown into the river—even from its "corpse," which is still preserved in the attic of the synagogue, emanates fear and dread, and it must, therefore, not be looked upon.

Always, in all these legends, the Golem is utilized for the protection of persecuted Jews, at such junctures when mere human strength and wisdom alone are no longer effectual.

Is it a symbol of God's help, which always comes in due season, although frequently (like the Golem) at the last, most anxious moment?

The ultimate madness of the Golem, this so startling denouement of all the legends, does not necessarily contradict this interpretation. It may simply be a foreign *motif* which, because of external similarity, became amalgamated with these legends. The *motif* of the "spirits, which he conjured up, from which he could never free himself," which, as was the case with the Golem of Kholm, ultimately overmastered those who created them.

It is also possible, however, to explain this denouement along the lines of the foregoing interpretation, without the assumption of a foreign *motif,* and in this way: That the help of God upon which man ultimately comes to depend supinely and thoughtlessly, brings about his ruin, because the "Holy One" comes to spurn such spiritless men.

Whatever it be, no one has yet been able to fathom the probable meaning of the Golem legends. Even these hints do not give any key to the mystery. But perhaps there are in the present book significant tales which may inspire a more profound interpretation of these unusually noteworthy legends.

Rabbi Loew made use of the Golem as an intelligencer, principally for the purpose of exposing "ritual" murder accusations against Jews and to apprehend the instigators of these libels. This so-called blood accusation continues to crop up from time to time; but the Golem, too, appears with all his supernatural might, with spectral power, in various forms, and rises up against the greatest lie of the centuries; he is to be met with everywhere, but most frequently where he is least expected. . . .

We have all heard of the Golem in our childhood years, and since then it has become indelibly engraved upon our memories. In recent times, he has attained so-to-speak European celebrity, because contemporary writers and artists have been interesting themselves in him. With defiant fury, he has broken through the walls of the Ghetto, and now stands on guard for the world. His voice is to be heard complaining of the sorrows of our own day, which are shared also by the ancient Jewish race.

THE BIRTH OF JUDAH LOEW

ON the first Seder night in the year of the world, 5273 (C. E. 1513), a son was born to the higly revered rabbi of the old city of Worms on the Rhine, Bezalel ben Hayim, descendant of Rav Hai Gaon, scion of the seed of David in the male line.

The very birth of the child brought to his community, nay, to the entire Jewish people, miraculous rescue from a great misfortune.

The world knows well to what bitterness and persecution the Jews of Europe, and especially of Germany, were subjected because of the old lie which always kept cropping up that they utilize the blood of Christians in their Passover feast. This accusation would spread like the plague through town and country, and scarcely a Passover went by that the corpse of a Christian was not smuggled into some synagogue yard or into the cellar of some leader of the community, in order to provide a pretext for breaking loose against the Jews, for the enhancement of God's name and the honor of the Christian faith.

This is what happened on that Passover eve upon which Rabbi Loew first saw the light of the world.

It was the "night of watching" *Lel Shimurim* (see Exod. XII, 42). The Jews of the ghetto were celebrating the feast of emancipation, that ancient festival which stands guard over the memory of a time when an enslaved race awoke to the realization of having arrived at nationhood.

There is no people for whom its religious and national festivals have such significance as theirs have for the Jews; to no people are its festivals such a source of courage and consolation as are their festivals to the Jews. For to them must their holidays supply a large part of what other nations derive from their everyday existence.

And that is why every Jewish holiday is to the Jews just like an oasis in the so dreary and terror-full desert of their exile—an oasis which strengthens and refreshes them and gives them new energy to bear the burden of their sufferings.

And for this reason the festivals of the Jews are never more welcome, never more beatifying than just at times of great danger, of redoubled anxiety and dread.

No Jewish festival, regarded from this point of view, is so significant as the Feast of Passover. Not only is the fact of emancipation itself the characteristic foundation of Jewish history. The manner of salvation has also remained the same. The rescue always came about, as it did in Egypt, in the moment of greatest need and always in the form of wonders.

It was a beautiful night. Silently the moon floated through the clear heavens, and the little stars were smiling and greeting with their soft rays.

Without, all was still; the Jew's street was as silent as the grave; but from the windows glowing lights poured upon the unpeopled streets.

Every Jew was seated at the Seder-table, covered with its white cloth and set with the flat, unleavened cakes, the bitter herbs, the red wine, and the glowing candles; each one was reading with touching sincerity and deep devotion the *Haggadah*, the history of the exodus from Egypt,

40

and was enumerating the plagues which the Eternal had visited upon the Egyptians, the tyrants, and oppressors of the Jews. The *paterfamilias* takes the bitter herbs, the *maror*, shows it to his table-companions, and recites in a loud voice: "Why do we eat of the bitter herbs?— Because the Egyptians embittered our lives."

Especially beautiful were the Seder festivities in the house of Rabbi Bezalel, of the highly revered divinely gifted scholar of his community, to which, true to the words of the *Haggadah*, "He who is hungry come and eat!" many poor, homeless coreligionists had been invited to the table, and added to the joyful spirit of the celebration.

With enthusiasm the psalms and sacred songs which have been purposefully collected for this evening were chanted. Especially touching was the prayer of thanksgiving.

"We, therefore, are in duty bound to thank, praise, adore, glorify, extol, honor, bless, exalt and reverence Him, Who wrought all these wonders for our ancestors and for us; He brought us forth from bondage unto freedom; from sorrow unto joy, from mourning unto festivity; from darkness unto great light, and from servitude unto redemption; and therefore let us chant unto Him a new song. Hallelujah!"

And when the door was opened for "the reception of Elijah the Prophet," Rabbi Bezalel recited with burning devotion, loud and strong, almost imperiously:

"O pour out Thy wrath upon the heathen that have not known Thee, and upon the kingdoms that have not called upon Thy name. For they have devoured Jacob, and laid waste his dwelling place. Pour out Thine indignation upon them, and let Thy wrathful anger take hold of them. Persecute and destroy them in anger from under the heavens of the Eternal."

And just as the melodious litany "And it came to pass at midnight" was intoned, groans and moans of pain were audible. The good, pious wife of Rabbi Bezalel, who was about to be confined, was overtaken by birth pangs. Several persons ran quickly into the street in order to call a midwife.

At the same moment there was approaching the house of Rabbi Bezalel a man, completely wrapped in a shawl, and carrying a bundle on his shoulders. Despite the nocturnal darkness of the narrow street, he strode forward with the firm step of one who was sure of his way.

When, however, he caught sight of the people coming out of the house of Rabbi Bezalel, he slunk quickly into a side street and took to his heels.

The night-patrol who saw the man with the bundle and those who were running from the house of Rabbi Bezalel, guessed that it was a case of a runaway thief, captured the man and brought him to the city magistrate.

There it was established that the man had the corpse of a child concealed in the bundle. It may be imagined what a figure that man cut—certainly not a graceful one. In order to divert suspicion of murder from himself, he made no secret of the fact that he had been hired by several Christian citizens, whom he named, to smuggle the corpse of a Christian boy who had died on the preceding day into the cellar of Rabbi Bezalel. Thereupon the entire crew was clapped into jail during the course of the same night.

During the morning service on the first day of Passover, prayers of thanks were recited. Rabbi

Bezalel delivered a sermon which was introduced by this prayer from the *Haggadah:*

"And it is this same promise which hath been the support of our ancestors and of us as well; for not one only hath risen up against us, to annihilate us, but in every generation hath an adversary risen against us to destroy us, but the Holy One, blessed be He, delivered us out of their hands."

At the feast of the circumcision, Rabbi Bezalel said:

"The child is our people's comforter. He has come into the world in order to free us from the terrible blood-lie, the most ignominous calumny which we suffer."

He named the child Judah Loew, according to the Bible verse (Genesis XLIX, 9) "Judah is a lion's whelp; from the prey, my son, thou art gone up."

THE BETROTHAL

IN Worms itself, in those days, there was plenty of opportunity to become proficient in rabbinical learning, for did not the spirit of Rabbi Shelomo Jizhacki (Rashi), the great commentator of the Law, haunt the place? But it was the custom in those days for youths, following the words of the sages "Travel to a place of learning," to go abroad in order to sit at the feet of famous scholars and masters to quench their thirst for knowledge at every available spring.

Scarcely had he reached the age of adolescence, when Judah Loew traveled to Prague, in order to satisfy at the schools there his yearning for wisdom.

There lived in those days in Prague the rich and pious leader of the community, Reb Samuel Schmelke Reich, better known under the name

"Reich Schmelke." And when the latter wished to betroth his amiable and virtuous daughter Pearl, his choice fell upon none other than Loew. For in addition to the superior personal attractions of the latter, he also came of a family of noble lineage, with which Reb Schmelke, himself a child of Worms, was desirous of allying himself. Therefore, Loew was betrothed when scarcely fifteen years of age, according to the prevailing custom.

At the request of Reb Schmelke, Loew soon repaired to Poland to the famous school of Rabbi Solomon Luria of Lublin, who at that time was the star of the greatest magnitude in the heavens of Jewish learning, the supreme head of the Diaspora.

Soon thereafter, Reich suffered the loss of his entire fortune through a disasterous business venture, and was, therefore, not in position to raise the promised dowry or defray the cost of his daughter's wedding outfit. So he wrote Loew, who, in the meantime, had already reached the age of eighteen, a letter of the following tenor:

"Dear son: As, according to the advice of our sages, one should marry at eighteen, and as I am unable to give the dowry, I do not wish to hold you to your troth; we release you and you are at liberty to marry another woman."

To this Loew replied: "I trust in the help of God and will wait until He helps you to raise the dowry and the cost of the wedding outfit. Otherwise I will regard the troth as nullified only if you unite your daughter with another."

As the material condition of Reb Schmelke did not improve, Pearl set herself up in a store where bread, salt, and other food-stuffs were sold, in order to help her parents in their time of need.

Almost ten years passed. Loew was faithful to his troth, did not marry, but gave himself entirely to the study of science. For this reason he was called "Loew, the Bachelor."

One day, troops of soldiers marched through the streets of Prague. At their head rode an officer of high rank. As he came before Pearl's store, he impaled with his sword a large loaf of bread which was lying on the counter.

Pearl was terrified and screamed. She soon regained her poise, however, and begged the officer not to take the bread without paying for it, because she was supporting her aged parents out of the meagre profits of her little shop.

Her words did not leave the officer unmoved. He pulled the saddle from under him and threw it into the store, saying:

"I am hungry, but have no money to pay for the bread, so take the saddle instead!" Thereupon he rode away.

Pearl's patience and trust in God did not remain unrequited.

How astonished was she, to find upon taking the saddle in her hands, that it held a large number of gold ducats!

She ran swiftly home. With tears of joy she told her parents of the treasure which had come to her in so wonderful a manner.

Then Reb Schmelke Reich opined that the officer had been none other than Elijah the Prophet, and that this new turn of fortune was due to the great merits of his future son-in-law.

Of course, he at once informed Loew how Heaven had remembered him with kindness and had sent him help in a miraculous manner. He

48

begged him to come at once to Prague in order to have his marriage solemnized.

Loew came to Prague, married his pious bride, and it was not very long before he was called to occupy the position of Rabbi in the community of Posen.

RABBI LOEW AND THE CARDINAL OF PRAGUE

BETWEEN the time of his marriage and his being called to the rabbinate of Posen, Rabbi Loew became famous as one of the greatest rabbinical scholars. And when the ancient and respected Jewish community of Prague had to look about for a spiritual chief, the choice fell upon Rabbi Loew.

Prague had been called "a mother in Israel" since ancient times. Here Rabbi Loew found a wished-for ground to occupy himself, immediately upon coming into office, with a highly successful activity, and especially because of his linguistic knowledge, he also became renowned outside of the Jewish world. Christian scholars like the two astronomers, Tycho Brahe and John Kepler, were among his most intimate friends.

The Jews of Prague were at that time leading

a thorny existence. The hand of the Catholic ecclesiastics weighed heavily upon them, and they were given over to the mercies of the incited populace. In this city also, Jews suffered most from the superstitious blood accusation. One priest especially, Thaddeus by name, a fanatical Jew-hater, was untiring in his attempts to change peace and harmony into hatred and discord.

Rabbi Loew therefore considered it necessary to have a conference with the ecclesiastics in order to convince them of the baseness of all those calumnies against the Jews. He addressed to Johann Silvester, the Cardinal of Prague, a comprehensive memorandum which began with these words: *"I demand justice for my oppressed brethren."* He made it clear that it is a sin against God, against humanity, and against the teachings of Christ, to accuse the Jews of the use of Christian blood or to persecute them, on the ground of other preposterous lies. He requested that the Cardinal give him the opportunity to hold a disputation with the priesthood.

This memorial did not fail to make a deep impression.

The Prince of the Church answered that he

welcomed the suggestion and would arrange a disputation for the purpose outlined by Rabbi Loew.

Soon after, the Cardinal assembled about three hundred priests and theologians in order to lay down the basis of the debate and to decide upon the questions that were to be put. The agreement that was arrived at was communicated to Rabbi Loew. He informed the Cardinal, through a second communication, that it would be impossible for him as a single individual to debate with three hundred ecclesiastics at one time, and he, therefore, requested that arrangements be made for thirty conferences to be held on thirty days, and that upon each day ten of the priests were to put their questions in writing and hand them to the Cardinal, who would in turn transmit them to Rabbi Loew, who would answer them also in writing. This proposition was agreeable to the Cardinal who made the arrangements suggested.

In the meantime Rabbi Loew gave orders that during all the days of the disputation the Jews of Prague should recite special prayers in their synagogues and houses of worship.

THE DISPUTATION

MORE than one hundred questions were laid before Rabbi Loew. His brilliant and dignified explanations were greeted with unmixed admiration. Both the questions put to him by the priests and the answers of Rabbi Loew are to be found in a memorandum book which is still preserved in the archives of the Dominican Order in Prague.

Of the questions which were taken up the most important and interesting and Rabbi Loew's answers to them, follow:

1. According to the Talmud, do the Jews need the blood of Christians for their Passover festival?

The use of blood is forbidden by the Holy Scriptures. The Talmud neither cancelled nor modified this command; on the other hand the

Talmud made it more strict. Those sages who have taught: "Whoever raises his hand against his neighbor even if he does not strike him is an evil-doer" (Sanhedrin 58 b), and "Somewhat greater is the value of human beings, for in order to keep them alive even the commandments of the Torah may be suspended" (Beracoth 19 b), surely could not have authorized the use of human blood, especially when even the blood of animals is forbidden.

2. Are the Jews guilty of the crucifixion of Christ?

A King had an only son who had enemies in the capital who brought against him the accusation of *lese majeste*. The King's son was called to account for this and, upon the strength of the law, was condemned to die. The King was convinced of the innocence of his son but left him to his fate because the son had not uttered a single word in his own defense, and, as the judges pronounced the sentence, the condemned appealed to the King, "O help, father, you are surely convinced of my innocence! Rescue me from the hands of this band of murderers!" But the King

54

remained silent, and he was also an eye-witness of the execution; he did nothing to hinder it.

Now, who was to blame for the judicial crime? Was it the judges who, upon the ground of an accusation supported by evidence, condemned the man and ordered his execution, or was it the father, the King, from whom a mere word was sufficient to save his son from death?

There is nobody who can be made responsible for the execution of the son but the King himself. Whoever, however, gives expression to the opinion that the son was *unjustly* executed becomes guilty himself of *lese majeste* for he doubts the love of justice of the King.

Consider your own teachings on this subject. According to them, Jesus Christ died on the cross to save humanity, to do penance for its sins; he must, according to your doctrines, have suffered a tragic death with all its bitterness and indignity, in order to return as a sacrifice to his father. It had to be so, it was the unsearchable and inscribable decree of God.

So he had to die. And by whose hands did he have to die? By the hands of his own brothers who were God's people and called so by him.

If they had not killed him they would have disobeyed God's word, God's command. They had to kill him.

God, the creator of all creatures, willed it so. Christendom owes thanks to the Jews for the crucifixion of Jesus. For, how could Christianity with all its basic doctrines have originated, how could it continue to exist if its founder had not been a martyr?

Therefore the Jews are not guilty of the death of Jesus, and it is, upon your part, ingratitude toward them and an offense against God if you try to revenge yourselves upon them for the crucifixion of Jesus.

It is also important to note that it was not the rabbinical Jews, the Pharisees or the Essenes, who accused Jesus, but the Saducees who were at war with the rabbis and, together with King Herod were Roman partisans. The sentence was delivered by the Roman government, it was carried out by Romans. This is shown by the manner of execution because crucifixion was a form not known to the Talmud and, what is more, was introduced by the Romans.

3. *Is the Jew according to the Talmud advised to hate Christians?*

A king had officers of various ranks. In accordance with this order of ranks, each class had to show respect for the higher classes. This is not the case, however, where the king is concerned, for all, without respect to rank, must show him honor. If, however, one of them, unmindful of the presence of the king, shows honor to his superior, does he not by so doing violate the majesty of the king?

Now, in the Talmud there are many passages which speak of non-Jews with contempt, but these passages concern only those non-Jews who serve not God, but his subjects, the sun and various planets. Those non-Jews who worship God are not meant! On the contrary, there are to be found in the Talmud and in later Jewish writings many passages in which Jews are commanded to respect righteous *heathens* and even more so non-Jews who believe in God. "The righteous of all nations have a share in the world to come," says the Talmud *(Tosefta Sanhedrin xiii, 2).* In another place it says: "Pious heathens who serve God are equal to priests" *(Otiot de Rabbi Akiba, Ch. 13)*. Again, "He who honors the Divinity in any righteous manner whatsoever, even if his belief is different from ours, should be treated the same as a Jew." *(Rabbi Menachem Meiri's "Schita Mekubezet" to Baba Kamma 113b)*. Rabbi Eliezer, son of Samuel Halevi, who died in 1357 in Mayence, wrote in his "Testament": "Those who lie to non-Jews or overreach them belong to the class of those who desecrate the name of God." Others have taught: "To deceive non-Jews is strictly forbidden." *(Tana d'bei Elijahu, Ch. 28)*. "It is entirely unlawful to overreach a non-Jew, for it is written: It is an abomination before God to commit a wrong."

4. Why is the converted Jew despised by his former co-religionists?

Each king has various kinds of soldiers—infantry, cavalry, marines, royal bodyguards, etc. All are expected to serve their highest war commander. But it is regarded as desertion, severely punished according to the laws of war, if a soldier goes over from one branch of the service to another, and the comrades whose battle flag he

58

leaves despise him just as if he had gone over to
the enemy.

5. *Why do the Jews exalt themselves as the
"Chosen People"?*

A king ordered two regiments to come to his
residence city. To the one he gave difficult duties
and imposed severe restrictions, the other received very easy work and many liberties.

Once a quarrel arose between the Colonels of
the two regiments. One claimed that his regiment
was regarded by the king with greater favor than
was the other, it was preferred by the king and
had therefore been given the most difficult tasks;
its members were foremost in the service of the
king. To the other regiment, however, he had
not given any important duties, because he had
no confidence in it. But the other Colonel maintained the contrary view that *his* regiment was
preferred by the king and was therefore given
little work to do.

The matter came to the knowledge of the king,
who gave out this command: "You must not
quarrel as to which regiment stands higher in
my favor; both serve me, and there is no question

of any preference. As for the question, however, with which regiment I am more satisfied—that you shall learn upon your departure hence, when it will be shown who will receive the greater distinction."

The election of Israel constitutes no priority of rights, no favored special statuts, but is, on the contrary, a difficult moral obligation, entailing tremendous responsibilities. To fulfill the mission of high which lies in the teachings given at the Burning Bush is not easy. By accepting the teachings of God, Israel was elected by God to be unto all peoples the pathfinder to the idea of pure divinity, and whenever he has stumbled or gone astray, he has been severely enough punished. God laid upon the Jews a large measure of difficult duties as the price of this election and demanded of them great severities toward themselves. He choses a people in order to entrust them with a great, difficult life-work, while he left the other peoples to go peacefully on their way. So says the prophet: "You only have I known of all the families of the earth; therefore I will visit upon you all your iniquities." (*Amos iii, 2*). Another says: "Hearken to my voice and do them (the words of God's covenant) according to all which I command you; so shall ye be My people, and I will be your God." *(Jeremiah xi, 4).* True to the doctrine expressed in these words, there is to be found in the Talmud and in later Jewish writings the view that the election of Israel depends solely upon the will to belong to God. Thus, Rabbi Meir teaches: "The non-Jew who occupies himself with the law, is equal to the High Priest. For it is written: 'Observe my precepts and commandments which man should practice so that he may live.' It does not say that priests, Levites or Israelites shall live by them, but every man." *(Talmud Babli, Aboda Zara 3a).* Rabbi Samuel Bar Nachmani says: "God made a covenant with Israel only for the sake of the law." *(Yalkut to Psalm 319).* The word of the Eternal "If ye will hearken unto My voice indeed, and keep my covenant, then ye shall be Mine own treasure from among all peoples. . . . And ye shall be unto Me a kingdom of priests and a holy nation." *(Exod. xix 5-6)* is thus construed: "You must serve Me only and completely, devote yourselves to the law and to no other thing." *(Midrash Yalkut Jethro, 276).*

Significant is also the reply which our great lawcommentator Moses ben Maimon gave to the proselyte Obadiah who asked whether he had the right to use in prayer the expression "God of our fathers," the fathers whom God had chosen in ancient times. Rabbi Moses answered with all positiveness that the proselyte, be he even of heathen descent, may regard himself as a descendant of Abraham, for here it is not a question of physical descent but of spiritual, and this includes all men who abandon idolatry and all the sins bound up with it and cleave to God. "Unto the end of days, those among the non-Jewish peoples who acknowledge God, can count himself among the descendants of Abraham, for Abraham was not only the first ancestor of his physical descendants, but the father of all those human beings who choose the path of virtue. Abraham is, therefore, no less the father of thee, proselyte Obadiah, than of me: he is the father of all the righteous." (Maimonides, *Responsa I, 158*).

That the Jews do not look upon their "chosenness" as something belonging to them alone, is most clearly shown by the fact that on the "dreadful days," New Year's and Atonements Day, the Jews pray to God "that all created beings may unite in one covenant."

The astute and wise answers of Rabbi Loew were received by all his auditors with applause. The Cardinal pressed his hand in a friendly manner and said to him: "Your answers are very valuable to me. I shall show you at once my recognition by reporting to all the priests in my dominion the disputation and the satisfactory answers to our questions. I hope that from this time on peace and harmony will prevail between the adherents of both faiths."

The three hundred priests who participated in the disputation also pledged their friendship to Rabbi Loew.

THE MAKING OF THE GOLEM

THE favorable outcome of Rabbi Judah Loew's disputation with the ecclesiastics of Prague was a comfort in those troublous times to the Jews of that city who began to hope for a brighter future. But the fanatical priest Thaddeus continued to attempt mischief. Besides incitatory sermons, he was restlessly seeking, together with others of his frame of mind, to spread the blood accusation against the Jews and to mislead Jewish girls in order to influence them to accept the Christian belief.

Rabbi Loew thus expressed himself to his pupils: "I fear this Thaddeus for his soul is a spark of Goliath the Philistine giant. I hope, however, to subdue him, for my soul is a spark of the Jewish youth and later king, David. We must, nevertheless, all bend our entire spiritual energies to the end that we may not become his victims."

64

It was the year 5340 (1580).

Thaddeus strained every nerve to succeed in bringing forward a "ritual" murder charge against the Jews of Prague.

Rabbi Loew learned of this in time and directed a dream-question to Heaven, asking to be counselled as to the manner and means wherewith to combat this wicked foe.

He received the following answer in words in alphabetical order:

Ato Bra Golem Devuk Hakhomer V'tigzar Zedim Chevel Torfe Yisroel.

"Make a Golem of clay and you will destroy the entire Jew-baiting company."

Rabbi Loew arranged these words in accordance with the *Zirufim* (formulas) laid down in the *Sefer Yezirath* (Book of Creation), with the result that he was filled with the conviction that he would be able, with the help of the letters revealed to him from Heaven, to make a living body out of clay.

He sent for his son-in-law, Isaac ben Simson, who was a *Kohen* (priest), and for his pupil, Jacob ben Chayim Sasson, who was a *Levi* (Levite), and confided to them the mysterious manner in which he hoped to be able to make the Golem.

Rabbi Loew said: "I wish to make a Golem, and I bespeak your colaboration because for this creative act the four elements, *Aysch, Mayim, Ruach, Aphar* (fire, water, air and earth) are necessary. Thou, Isaac, art the element of fire; thou, Jakob, art the element of water; I, myself, am air; working together, we shall make out of the fourth element, earth, a Golem."

Rabbi Loew, thereupon, gave them the minutest instructions how they must before all, through deep, earnest penitence, sanctify and purify themselves, in order to be prepared for the exalted work of creating a being of stone. He also pointed out to them the danger in which the three of them might be placed if, by reason of incomplete inner sanctification, the attempt would fail, for they would then have used the Holy name in vain, or desecrated it.

On the second day of the month of Adar, after midnight, the three men betook themselves to the *Mikveh* (the ritual bath of the Jews), immersed themselves this time with special reverence, then repaired to Rabbi Loew's house where they chanted the *Hazoth,* the midnight lament for Jerusalem, and in deepest devotion recited the appropriate Psalms. They then took out the *Sefer Yezirah,* from which Rabbi Loew read several chapters aloud. Finally, they wended their way to the outskirts of the city, to the banks of the Moldau. There, they sought and found a clay-bed and at once set to work. . . .

By torch-light and amidst the chanting of Psalms, the work was begun with feverish haste.

They formed out of clay the figure of a person, three ells in length, and with all members. And the Golem lay before them with his face turned toward heaven.

The three men then placed themselves at its feet, so that they could gaze fully into its face.

It lay there like a dead body, without any movement.

Then, Rabbi Loew bade the *Kohen* walk seven times around the clay body, from right to left, confiding to him the *Zirufim* (charms) which he was to recite while doing this.

When this was done, the clay body became red, like fire.

Then Rabbi Loew bade the Levite walk the

same number of times, from left to right, and taught him also the formulas suitable to his element. As he completed his task, the fire-redness was extinguished, and water flowed through the clay body; hair sprouted on its head, and nails appeared on the fingers and toes.

Then Rabbi Loew himself walked once around the figure, placed in its mouth a piece of parchment inscribed with the *Schem* (the name of God); and, bowing to the East and the West, the South and the North, all three recited together: *"And he breathed into his nostrils the breath of life; and man became a living soul."* (Genesis ii, 7.)

And the three elements, Fire, Water, and Air, brought it about that the fourth element, Earth, became living. The Golem opened his eyes and looked, astonished, about him.

And Rabbi Loew said to him: "Stand up!" And he stood up.

Then they dressed him in the garments of a *Shammes* (sexton) and he was soon, to all appearances, an ordinary person; only the faculty of speech was lacking to him, for those words which Heaven had confided to him did not

68

possess the power to control those *Zirufim* which could have endowed the Golem with speech. And that was really an advantage. God knows what could have happened if a Golem had been given the faculty of speech also!

At daybreak, *four* men went homeward.

On the way, Rabbi Loew thus addressed the Golem: "Know thou that we have formed thee from a clod of earth. It will be thy task to protect the Jews from persecution. Thou shalt be called Joseph and thou shalt lodge in the home of the Rabbi. Thou, Joseph, must obey my commands, when and whither I may send thee—in fire and water; or if I command you to jump from the housetop, or if I send thee to the bed of the sea!"

Joseph nodded in token of assent.

Arrived home, Rabbi Loew told how he had found the dumb stranger upon the street, that he had compassion upon him and had engaged him as rabbinical bodyservant. But Rabbi Judah forbade the members of his household to send the Golem upon private or secular errands.

THE GOLEM AS WATER CARRIER

THE wife of Rabbi Loew could not, however, understand why her husband had forbidden the use of the Golem for private purposes. And when, just before Passover, she was short of help she allowed herself to give the Golem orders to fill the two large water kegs which stood in the kitchen which was all prepared for the holiday. She thought also that a service in preparation for the Passover feast did not come under the head of secular purposes.

But she had a very unpleasant experience.

The Golem took the pails and ran swiftly to the brook.

Several hours later the courtyard of the house of the Rabbi was flooded with water, and people were crying: "Water! Water!" The secret source from which this water was flowing was sought.

70

But is was not found until the Golem was seen patiently obeying his orders by continuing to pour water into the kegs which had been filled a long time before. This explained the flood and there was much laughter over the Golem's mistake.

Rabbi Loew said to his wife jestingly: "You have certainly found an excellent water carrier for the holidays. If you had only explained to him that he should stop when the kegs were full!"

The Golem, however, entirely unconcerned by the episode, continued his work and went again to the brook to get water. Then Rabbi Loew exclaimed, "Enough! Enough water!" and the Golem at once put down the pails.

Since that time the people took care not to give the Golem any profane work to do. To this very day in Prague people say to an unskilled artisan: "You are as competent for this work as was Joseph Golem as water carrier!"

THE GOLEM AS FISHERMAN

ONCE, before the New Year holidays, Rabbi Loew himself was compelled to make use of the Golem for private purposes.

It was during a terrible storm. A veritable hurricane was blowing, and the rain was coming down in torrents. It was therefore impossible for fishermen to go out for their catch, and in the entire city of Prague not a single fish was to be had.

Rabbi Loew, however, did not wish to be without fish on the holiday and decided to send the Golem fishing, because he knew that the stormy weather would be no hindrance to him.

As there was no suitable basket handy, the Golem was given a grain sack. Rabbi Loew instructed him how to use the net and how to put the fish that were caught into the sack, and told him to come home soon.

72

The Golem at once repaired to the river, entirely unconcerned by the weather. As to the meaning of the word "soon" he had not the slightest idea.

In the meantime, a man from a neighboring village brought the Rabbi a very fine fish, so that the Golem and his errand were entirely forgotten.

It was, however, Rabbi Loew's custom on the afternoon preceding the Sabbath or a festival, to give the Golem instructions as to what he was to do during the rest day. When, therefore, he asked that the Golem be sent to him he was reminded that the Golem had been ordered to go fishing in the morning.

Rabbi Loew at once sent the aged *Shammes*, Abraham Chayim, to call the Golem home. He told him that, in case the Golem would show him that he had not yet caught any fish, he was to say to him: "The Rabbi doesn't care for the fish and wants you to come home at once!" Quickly the *Shammes* went to the river and there found the Golem standing right in the raging current of water just on the point of sinking the net again.

Abraham Chayim called to him: "The Rabbi wants you to come home at once!"

But the Golem showed him by raising the sack that this was not yet full.

Then Abraham Chayim shouted: "Joseph, the Rabbi said that he doesn't care for your fish and that you can come home without any!"

When the Golem heard this, he quickly shook the fish out of the bag into the water and ran home.

When Rabbi Loew was told about this he laughed and said to his people: "Now I see that the Golem is fit only for sacred purposes and should not be employed to do profane things."

Since that time people were even more careful than before not to send the Golem upon ordinary errands.

THE GOLEM IS GIVEN WORK

FROM this time on, Rabbi Loew utilized the services of the Golem only in such cases as involved the clearing up of some threatened accusation against Judaism. Whenever he entrusted him with a misson which was likely to be dangerous, Rabbi Loew would provide the Golem with an amulet which made him invisible.

In this condition the Golem went among the Jewbaiters and listened to their conversations. If he learned of any evil designs, he would come quickly to Rabbi Loew and the peril that threatened would be averted in time.

From year to year, in the time between Purim and Passover, when blood accusations against the Jews were frequently made, the Golem, in the costume of a Christian porter, used to loiter about, night after night, in the streets of the ghetto. As soon as he perceived any suspicious figure, especially if he carried a bundle or was driving a wagon, the Golem would quickly approach and make a thorough investigation. If the suspicious person was found to have a dead child in his possession, the Golem would drag him by force to the authorities and, after calling attention to the culprit by means of various gestures, disappear.

In this way the Golem became the terror of the enemies of the Jews. Some regarded him as a spectre of Rabbi Loew.

THE GOLEM IS REPORTED

AT about this time, there lived in Prague the famous philanthropist and communal leader, Mordecai Meisel. A Christian butcher by the name of Havlicek owed him five thousand gulden, for which Meisel was compelled to sue him. Havlicek thought of a means for having Meisel put into prison, knowing that there Meisel would forget his demands.

The time of the Passover feast arrived. Havlicek decided to smuggle the corpse of a child into the house of Mordecai Meisel, and then to report to the authorities that Meisel was implicated in the murder of a child.

In those days, the slaughter house was situated on the other side of the Jews' street, so that Christian butchers also used it as a thoroughfare.

Havlicek went about his work in the following manner: He opened the grave of a child who had but recently died, took the corpse with him into the slaughter house, where, in a remonte corner, he made an incision in its throat to make it appear that the child had been "ritually" slaughtered, covered it with a small prayer shawl, and placed it inside of a slaughtered pig.

It was a dreadfully dark night, as if God had poured blackness over everything in the world. About midnight Havlicek placed the pig upon a waggon and, driving noiselessly toward the Jewish quarter, was on the point of throwing the corpse of the child cautiously through the cellar window of the house of Mordecai Meisel, but "behold, He that keepeth Israel does neither slumber nor sleep." (Psalms cxxi, 4.)

After the Golem had, faithful to the command of his master, peered into the darkness of the night, watching out for suspicious persons, he caught, sight of a waggon, upon the box of which a man was driving. A waggon . . . ? In a wink, he was there, making a thourough search. When he came upon the bundle in the carcass of the slaughtered pig, he quickly took the reins and bound Havlicek fast to the driver's seat. The latter, himself a man of athletic build, tried with

all the strength of a desperate man to defend
himself and struggled with his assailant. When,
however, the latter had given him several hard
blows so that he began to bleed, the desire to
fight abandoned him, and, like an animal caught
in a trap, he left off struggling. Thereupon the
Golem became driver and rode at a rapid pace
directly to the office of the city magistrate.
Aroused by the rumbling of a waggon and the
groans of Havlicek, the sheriffs hurried out and
freed the victim, Havlicek speechless and bewildered. By the light of torches, the waggon was
searched to find out what the nocturnal prowler
had stolen from his victim, and in this way the
corpse of the child wrapped up in a prayer shawl
was found. When Havlicek finally recovered
from his terror, he truthfully answered questions
put to him and swore that he had not murdered
the child.

The Golem, however, had long since disappeared.

On the following morning the story of the
singular detective spread rapidly through the
entire city.

This episode served to increase the antagonistic

attitude of the Priest Thaddeus against Rabbi Loew. He guessed that Rabbi Loew had had a hand in the occurrence and had employed mysterious powers. He therefore spread the rumor that Rabbi Loew was a sorcerer.

THE RENEGADE

IN the year 5343 (1583) a perilous storm cloud
loomed over the Jews of Prague; a dreadful
danger threatened them. During the inter-
mediate days of Passover, a Jewish girl by the
name of Dinah, the daughter of the surgeon,
Maridi, who was himself but loosely attached to
the race and the religion of his fathers, left her
home with the object of becoming a Christian.
She betook herself to the Priest Thaddeus, who
rejoiced exceedingly over this unhoped-for catch.
This incident would in itself have been of no
consequence, because in Jewish circles there was
always rejoicing when such rotten fruit fell from
the tree. But because another incident which
took place in Prague at the same time and in
those dark days could have led to dreadful consequences, this conversion obtained increased
significance.

A Christian girl who was in the service of one of the most eminent Jews of Prague and who in winter also performed the function of a *Shabbos-Goya,* suddenly disappeared from the ghetto. Her employer, who had come to be very much dissatisfied with her, thought nothing of her departure, and assumed that she was staying with her relatives, whose name she did not know, in a small village not far from Prague.

But Thaddeus learned of the matter and considered it a favorable opportunity to incite the people to persecute the Jews of Prague, and his efforts had, thanks to circumstances, extremely good prospects of success.

To the renegade Jewess, even before the conversion was accomplished, fell an important task, namely, to cast the Jews of Prague into profound misery—she was to celebrate her conversion with the blood of her brethren. Thaddeus enlisted her confidential co-operation in the work he had undertaken, and she was quite ready and willing to swear falsely against her co-religionists. When, shortly following her departure from her home, she was brought before the Cardinal and the latter, as was the custom, asked Dinah why she wished to change her faith, she answered maliciously, with a satanic smile: "I am disgusted with the barbaric customs and the fanatical rites of the Jews. How can one remain in a religion whose followers, year in, year out, slaughter a Christian for the purpose of mixing his blood in their Passover bread?"

"I would like to ask you only one question, although I had really intended to put many to you," said the Cardinal. "How do you know" — the Cardinal spoke these words with a sharp, penetrating look — "that the Jews slaughter a Christian?" In answer to this question, Dinah told the following story:

"A few days before Passover, there came to my father two servants of a rabbi, the one old and short of stature, the other a black-bearded young man of medium height, who was, however, as I could see from the signs he made with his fingers, a deaf mute. The first said to my father: 'The rabbi of the community sends you a vial of Christian blood for the Passover.' My father gave him in turn for it a large contribution and commanded my mother to mix part of the Christian blood with the *matzoths* and part with the red wine to be used on Seder night. When I saw this, I was horrified and I made up my mind to forsake this accursed people and to seek salvation among those who were not consumers of blood."

The Cardinal thereupon asked her whether she knew how the Jews obtained a Christian for the purpose, and remarked, at the same time, that to his knowledge no reports of a missing person had been made to the authorities. To this Dinah replied: "I don't know anything about that. But in so far as I was able to understand the conversation of the rabbi's servant with my father, it must have been the *Shabbos-Goya*. For the old man said, upon parting, patting my father cheerfully on the shoulder: 'Don't worry, Reb Maridi; when winter comes, we will, with God's help, have a new *Shabbos-Goya*.'" Concluding she begged, with devilishly feigned innocence, that her father should be exempted from being called as a witness, because he would in that case fall a victim to the hatred of his co-religionists, and especially of the old rabbi.

The Cardinal, a noble and also clever man, was convinced that it was all a tissue of lies.

Nevertheless, it was his duty to report the testimony of the renegade Jewess and to refer the matter for investigation to the judicial authorities. He sent, however, confidentially a copy of the girl's statement to Rabbi Loew and advised him immediately to follow the threads of the lies, but especially to clear up the mysterious disappearance of the *Shabbos-Goya*. In the meantime, the scurrilous rumor spread like wildfire throughout the entire city and the Jews were thrown into the depths of care and worry.

When Rabbi Loew received the report and the letter of the Cardinal, he was deeply troubled. He read the testimony of the renegade Jewess several times with great attention, and it occurred to him that inasmuch as the affair was already known to the authorities, his two loyal servants, Abraham Chayim and the Golem, would be thrown into prison before nightfall. He began to consider what to do. It occurred to him that the would-be convert could hardly know Joseph Golem very well, and that, therefore, it was possible to seek a mute of similar appearance, dress him in the clothes of the Golem, and arrange that he should stay that night in the rabbinical office on the bed usually occupied by the Golem. Nobody knew the reason for this. Rabbi Loew commanded the Golem, dressed as a Christian porter, to remain as ever on the watch.

The shrewd calculations of the rabbi turned out to be correct. At nightfall several policemen broke into the house of Abraham Chayim, led him in manacles to prison, while others came into the Rabbi's house and did the same to the supposed deaf and dumb servant.

Rabbi Loew was very much perplexed by the course of events. He considered it as not impossible that steps might be taken for his own arrest, which would mean that any work to clear up the disappearance of the *Shabbos-Goya* would have to be abandoned. Upon his order, the anxious members of the community resorted to the synagogues and offered heartfelt and contrite prayers, appealing to God, with hearts full of pain, to save the bewildered community from the danger that threatened.

Several weeks went by, and despite all efforts, Rabbi Loew did not succeed in discovering the whereabouts of the *Shabbos-Goya*. Soon after, he received a summons to be present at the trial of

the two servants, Abraham Chayim and the
nameless mute. It was to begin three days before
Shevuoth. Only one month was left for clearing
up the mystery. Rabbi Loew was profoundly
worried.

* * *

Rabbi Loew was profoundly worried It is true
that it was not as one accused but as the represen-
tative of the community that he had been summoned, but he looked forward to the day of the
trial with trembling and anxiety. Well he knew
that if he did not in the meantime succeed in
clearing up the mystery of the disappearance of
the *Shabbos-Goya,* not only he but the entire
Jewish people and its sacred religion would be
dragged to the culprit's bench.

If he only knew of some way in which to have
the proceedings postponed in order to gain more
time! But there was absolutely no possibility of
doing this. He did not, therefore, allow the time
to go by without action.

He made secret inquiries through confidential agents in an endeavor to ascertain the whereabouts of the vanished *Shabbos-Goya.* But all

these attempts were fruitless. It was certain that she was living in one of the four villages in the vicinity of Prague. But the persons whom Rabbi Loew sent thither did not find her and came back empty-handed.

What was to be done? For the first time in his life, Rabbi Loew experienced perplexity and bewilderment. In vain he thought and thought on a plan of action. At last, he had resort to the Golem. He asked him if he had known the *Shabbos-Goya.* The Golem nodded affirmatively. Rabbi Loew then told him the entire story, and tried to impress upon him the dreadful doom which threatened the entire Jewish people if the *Shabbos-Goya* did not turn up in Prague before the trial. Then he commanded the Golem: "Thou, Joseph, must discover the *Shabbos-Goya,* wheresoever she may be; hand her this letter and bring her back without fail." He gave the Golem a letter in the name of the *Shabbos-Goya's* former mistress, who, of course, had no inkling of the epistle, which read as follows:

"The ring that was lost has been found. I beg your pardon a thousand times for having unjustly accused you. You were loyal to me, and

I did not act well toward you when I accused you of theft. I beg you, immediately upon receipt of this letter to come back to Prague with the bearer. The children, especially little Fanny, miss you very much and are looking to your early return. We will now know how to value you who have been so unusually good to us. We are sending you twenty-five gulden for traveling expenses.

"RACHEL."

Rabbi Loew dressed the Golem as a peasant and commanded him to set about his task without delay.

The day of trial approached, but no trace of either the Golem or the *Shabbos-Goya* appeared. Rabbi Loew was deeply troubled; he could scarcely conceal his anxiety. He gave orders that the day preceding the trial be observed as a strict fast-day and further that on the morning of the trial the entire community should assemble in the Altneu Synagogue in order to beseech the Almighty's mercy.

The day of the trial was a cloudy one, as if nature wished to show that it felt pity for the Jewish community in its time of trouble. Rabbi

Loew appeared at break of day in the synagogue where, just like on Yom Kippur (Day of Atonement), the entire congregation was assembled. He admonished them to repentence and to mutual forgiveness. After the solemn service, Rabbi Loew felt a new courage, and once more in possession of complete self-mastery which he needed so much at this critical moment.

The reverberating strokes of the bells from the church steeples announced that today was a great "religious day."

Before the courthouse a multitude was gathered. Soon the judges, preceded by a court attendant with a bundle of documents, strode with quick, excited strides into the courtroom. As Thaddeus, accompanied by the state witness, rode up, he was hailed by the populace with stormy acclamations.

A few minutes later, Rabbi Loew accompanied by Mordecai Meisel, the president of the community, appeared. They were received with cat-calls and whistling and cries of "Christ-killers!" It was only thanks to the precautions of the authorities that they were not trampled underfoot by the mob.

Then a bell announced the opening of the trial.

The crown-attorney, in earnest tones, read the accusation which charged the two rabbinical servants, Abraham Chayim and the nameless mute, with having perpetrated the murder of a Christian. He then asked the first of the accused whether it was true that, before the Passover, he had distributed Christian blood for use in the Passover bread.

Abraham Chayim answered humbly in a low but calm voice: "No!" Then came the turn of the other. The nameless deaf-mute.

The presiding judge took up some small vials, filled with a red liquid, and asked him whether he had carried such flasks. He nodded affirmatively with smiles of pleasure and put his finger to his mouth.

Thaddeus at once expressed the view that this man was confessing the truth, because by putting his finger to his mouth he was supplementing his answer by indicating that the liquid had been used for food. The Jew-haters among those present agreed with this view.

But the counsel for the accused opposed

this theory. Maintaining that the accused man believed that the bottles contained a kind of brandy, and that he thought that he was being asked if he wished to drink it. The lawyer then took a knife, placed it to his neck, pointed to Rabbi Loew and to the bottles and in this manner tried to ask the mute whether he had any knowledge of a murder and of the bottles.

The deaf-mute trembled. He became as white as chalk, nodded again and again in the negative, and with repeated gestures gave assurance that he knew nothing, absolutely nothing.

But Thaddeus declared that the accused believed that he was being asked if the Rabbi should be killed, and that was why he made these excited gestures. This gave rise to a heated dispute between Thaddeus and the counsel for the defense and the officiating judge felt called upon to admonish them both to come to order.

Then the chief witness, Dinah, was called. She looked all about the room, regarded the Rabbi with a scornful leer, and launched at once upon her ghastly and hideous testimony. She repeated exactly what she had told the Cardinal.

Then the defense counsel asked her: "Do you know well the servants of the Rabbi who came to your father with the phials of blood?"

Dinah pointed to the two accused and answered with complete assurance, laughing the while: "There they are. I would know them even in the dark!"

The demand of the defense that her father be called was denied because he had, in the meantime, left Prague and his present whereabouts were unknown.

For a moment a tense silence reigned in the courtroom. The crown counsel was just about to speak when, suddenly, through the open window, a loud noise was heard from the street.

A singular thing had happened. The Golem, the real mute servant of the Rabbi, appeared driving a waggon upon which sat a female—it was the *Shabbos-Goya!*

Joseph had with his Golem-instinct discovered her dwelling place in the nick of time; he had delivered to her the letter and the money, and she had decided at once to go with him to Prague. When Joseph had come to the Rabbi's house and had learned that the latter was attending the trial, he had bounded onto the wagon, and had ridden like one possessed to the courthouse. He had frightened the people who, believing that he would run over them, had cried out in terror.

When the judges inquired as to the cause of the uproar, they were told that the mute servant of the Rabbi and the *Shabbos-Goya* had arrived. The president ordered that they should both be summoned into the court forthwith.

As soon as Joseph Golem caught sight of the Rabbi he ran over to him joyfully and communicated to him, by means of his peculiar and unusual gestures, the success of his mission; at the same time he pointed to the *Shabbos-Goya*. All those present burst into a hearty laugh at his behavior.

Rabbi Loew's eyes shone with joy Thaddeus and Dinah stood stock still, motionless as mummies.

Thus was despicable, criminal calumny exposed.

Rabbi Loew related what steps he had taken to clear the matter up, and his report was received by the populace and the judges with the greatest attention.

Instead of the two accused men, Dinah was sentenced to six years' imprisonment. Thaddeus, profoundly humbled, slunk to his cloister.

The Jews of Prague celebrated Shevuoth which came three days after the trial with an enthusiasm they had never felt before.

A PASSOVER MIRACLE

IT was *Erev Pesach* in the year 5344 (1584). As Rabbi Loew, in the Altneu Synagogue of Prague, was intoning the prayers which usher in the Feast of Deliverance, he made an error. Instead of reading *umachalif es hazmanim* (and He changes the seasons) he read *umachamitz es hazmanim*, (and He sours the seasons). Rabbi Loew was frightened by this error. "Stop!" he thought to himself, "This must signify something special, perhaps an attack upon us!"

He broke off praying and, turning to the congregation, said:

"I must leave off praying, but you may go on, but no one must leave this place until I give the word."

He then called the old *shammas*, Abraham Chayim, and ordered him to go to all the other synagogues and tell the worshipers not to complete the service and not to leave until he would send word.

To the Golem, Rabbi Loew said: "Go quickly to my house and bring here one of the ordinary *matzoth* and one of the special *(mitzvah)* matzoth."

In a few minutes the Golem returned, his errand performed. Rabbi Loew asked him to taste first a piece of the ordinary *matzah* and then a piece of the *matzah shemurah* (special *matzah* used for the *Seder* ceremony, and throughout Passover by the very pious).

When he tasted the first *matzah*, the Golem indicated that it tasted good, but upon his biting into the *matzah shel mitzvah*, he became deathly pale, and indicated that he felt pain.

Rabbi Loew's countenance showed profound concern, and the congregation were filled with fear.

Poisoned Matzoth.

The face of the Golem became more and more distorted, he groaned and moaned, and Rabbi Loew felt compelled to relieve his pain by placing his hand on the Golem's body. The services of the supernatural creature were urgently needed.

The officials of the congregation stormed Rabbi

Loew with questions, but he gave no hint, but tried to allay their fears by saying: "Be of good cheer, brothers, God's help comes speedily, and He will save us from destruction." He then called the *shammes* and said: "Go into all the synagogues and, in my name, say that the *matzoth* which were baked in Prague (in those days, *matzoth* were also furnished to the city-dwellers by neighboring places) are to be regarded as *chometz* (leavened, ritually unfit) until I shall be able to satisfy my doubts as to their character. No one is even to touch one of these *matzoth*, especially children and sick persons. It is a matter of life and death!"

The Rabbi then called together all the men and women who had been connected with the preparation of the *matzoth* and asked if any non-Jew had worked with them. From them he learned that on the last day of the baking, fearing that the work would not be completed in time, they had called in two non-Jewish baker's apprentices, but that these had been busy entirely with the rodling (making the lines in the *matzoth* with a rodel, a toothed—wheel). The names of the two men were not known, although they were

98

well known in the Jewish quarter, where they were often employed to do miscellaneous work. They were generally referred to as "the red-beards."

Rabbi Loew, thereupon, gave instructions that only those *matzoth* which were baked on the previous day were under the ban, and that all others could be freely partaken of, on condition that they should be equitably divided, so that those whose *matzoths* belonged to the forbidden batch should have a supply. He then ordered that the services should be resumed and that each person should, upon their conclusion, go home and celebrate the *Seder*, without any more ado.

Rabbi Loew also went home but he did not sit down at the table. Again, he called the Golem, instructed him to go to the domicile of the "red-beards" and to look for any suspicious vials of liquid or packages of powder. He supplied the Golem with an amulet which rendered him invisible.

In a very short time, the Golem returned. He had not found either of the apprentices at home, and had had no difficulty in his search. In a drawer, he had come upon a little box of powder which he had brought back with him. When the Rabbi smelled the powder he noticed that it had the same odor as the *matzoth shel mitzvah*, but to a more concentrated degree. He then ordered the Golem to return at once to the apprentices' abode and to replace the box, exactly as he had found it. Accompanied by the *shammas*, Rabbi Loew then wended his way to the office of the prefect of police. On the way, the Rabbi and his companion met the "red beards" who could not conceal their surprise at the encounter. They greeted the Jews with a *"Gut Yomtov,"* being familiar with Jewish customs and expressions, and, after the rabbi and the *shammas* passed them, they remained standing, for some minutes, watching them.

The Investigation.

Rabbi Loew had difficulty in controlling himself, when, upon the inquiry of the chief of police as to what had brought him to the prefecture at so unusual an hour, he explained his errand. The chief listened, with wrapt attention, to the Rabbi's recital, and agreed with him that the finger of suspicion pointed to the two apprentices. He expressed his willingness personally to conduct an investigation without delay. Accompanied by two of his most skilled detectives, he proceeded to the home of the two suspects. Rabbi Loew, in the meantime, returned home in order to celebrate the Seder. It was already past midnight. Almost all the members of the congregation, who had completed the Seder, were assembled at his house, hoping to learn from him what had happened.

When the chief of police arrived at the abode of the apprentices, he did not find them at home. Hardly had the search begun when the detectives came upon the box of powder, more than half empty. The chief knew at once that it was poison, and it was clear to him that the two criminals must have mixed some of the powder in the flour used for *matzoth*. He at once sent the two detectives to seek the "red-beards", declaring that he would not leave the house until they were brought to him.

About an hour later, the detectives returned with the culprits, who wore hand-cuffs. The officers reported that the two miscreants had resisted arrest.

When the chief began to examine them, asking where they had procured the powder and what they had done with the portion missing from the box, the "red-beards" remained dumb, though their eyes showed that they were terrified.

The chief stamped his feet and said:

"If you confess the truth your punishment will be a mild one; if not, you may be put to death!"

The two exchanged looks, but remained silent.

Then the chief shouted in a tone which penetrated to the very marrow of their bones, and one of them felt compelled to make the following statement:

"We have been at home in the houses of Jews for a number of years. They have been very good to us. But sometime ago, we were sent for by the monk, Thaddeus, who said to us: 'It is quite probable that the Jews will need you as *Pesach-goyim* and that they will give you work. Well, do you wish to do something for which many will be very thankful to you?" We answered: 'Yes, we would be glad to do such a good deed.' Thereupon, he gave us a little vial containing a liquid and said: 'When you will be employed by the wine-seller Berger, try to pour into each barrel of wine a few drops of this liquid.' We said: 'We are not permitted to come near the wine.' Then he said: 'We must be through with the Jews once and for all, because their faith, their false faith is harmful. Therefore, you must do your very best to try to secure work in the *matzoth*-baking, and, if you do, be sure to drop this powder into the flour, especially in the flour which is being used for the *matzoth* of the Rabbi, who is a terrible sorcerer.' Saying this, he gave us the box of powder, promising us a large sum of money as a reward. So we asked the *matzoth* bakers to give us work, but they refused to do so until the day before the eve of the Passover when they sent for us. And, at a moment when we were unobserved, we threw part of the powder into the flour, but only part, because we were sorry to cause the death of so many people who had given us employment and the means of a livelihood for so many years."

Beware of a Red Beard.

It was dawn before the chief of police finished putting into writing this confession, which both miscreants were willing to sign. Rabbi Loew was then requested to instruct those Jews who had received the poisoned *matzoth* to bring these to the authorities who would need them as *corpora delicti*. During the morning services on the first day of Passover, announcement was made that all *matzoth* which had been baked on the day before *Erev Pesach* were to be delivered to the office of the chief of police. The Jews received this announcement with anxiety, as they could not understand what connection the authorities had with the *matzoth*.

In the meantime, police officers called upon the monk, Thaddeus, and examined him in an attempt to verify and confirm the statement of the apprentices. But Thaddeus denied the entire story, declared that he knew nothing about it, and offered to take an oath to that effect. Although they suspected him, the officers could not arrest Thaddeus, because they had no evidence besides the confession of the apprentices. These two, however, were each sentenced to five years imprisonment.

Since that day, the Jews of Prague have been careful never to let a "red-beard" come into

their homes, and the proverb is to this day current among them, "Beware of a red beard!"

On the seventh day of Passover, in the course
of a sermon on the wonderful redemption of the
Israelites from Egypt through the miraculous
parting of the Red Sea, Rabbi Loew told all
about the Providential rescue. He said: *"En baal
ha-nes makir b'nisso,*— those for whom Heaven
performs a miracle do not know of the greatness
of the miracle. Had I not, in reciting the prayers
on *Erev Pesach,* made an error, by saying
umachmiz instead of *umachalif* a dreadful calamity would have fallen upon our community!"

THE ROMAMCE OF RAHLE
AND LADISLAUS

IN those days, there lived in Prague a rich Jew by the name of Michael Berger, a man endowed with all the noble virtues of humanity, who always took pride in serving unselfishly the interests of his race and of his fatherland as well. Moreover he was a man who carried on his business, that of wine dealer, with unbending rectitude and punctilious honesty. In his home, peace and harmony prevailed.

He had an only daughter, Rahel. A more beautiful, more virtuous, more educated girl was not to be found in Prague. Despite her tender age—she was just seventeen—she helped to carry the burden of her father's business, representing him intelligently whenever he was occupied with the study of the Torah or with the interests of the community, of which he was one of the leaders. Sons of the most prominent Jews of Prague sought the hand of Rahel.

106

The peace of the Berger household did not last; it came to an end, alas, all too soon.

Among Berger's customers was Thaddeus, the fanatically anti-Jewish ecclesiastic. When he got to know Rahel there was born in him the determination to alienate her from her parents. It offended him that this gifted child should remain a lost soul. He wished to lead that soul to the salvation of the church.

On the pretext of adjusting what he claimed was an error in one of his monthly accounts, he insisted on personally examining the books of the wine dealer, knowing that Rahel was the bookkeeper. Irritated by Thaddeus' claim and anxious to defend her father's good name, Rahel, accompanied by a servant, repaired to Thaddeus' dwelling.

As she entered, he extended his hand and welcomed her with well simulated cordiality. He excused himself for troubling her, but he had found that he had been charged with ten bottles of wine which he did not remember having purchased.

A picture of a diligent business woman, Rahel produced all the order forms bearing his signature

which showed that her account was correct. As
if he now recalled something previously forgotten,
Thaddeus exclaimed:

"O, yes, you are right, young lady. But at the
same time, I am not wrong. The difference arises
because there were ten bottles of wine which were
of very bad quality, and which I, therefore, did
not include in my account. But I see now that
I must pay for these bottles because I failed to
return them and they are still in my possession."

Affronted by this remark, Rahel maintained
that it was impossible that the wine in these ten
bottles could be different from the rest.

"Courtesy forbids me to contradict you," said
Thaddeus regretfully. "I beg you, however, to
taste of the wine so that you may agree that
I have not gone to this trouble without cause."
He, thereupon, ordered a servant to fetch the
bottles from the cellar. When this had been done,
Thaddeus, laying his hand in a friendly manner
on Rahel's shoulder pointed to one of the bottles
and said:

"I have tasted the contents of this opened
bottle. As you, however, are not permitted to
drink of *yayn nesech* (wine that has been par-

taken of by a non-Jew) open another bottle and you will become convinced of the truth of my claim."

One can understand that Rahel did wish to be convinced. She had her servant open a flask and filled a goblet which Thaddeus held out to her. As the wine really was good, she drank the goblet dry.

"The wine is excellent! I do not understand why it does not suit your reverence," she said, confidently.

Thaddeus made a puzzled gesture, He also tasted the wine and confessed that it was good, but added that he was not surprised that good wine should be found in one of the bottles of the lot.

Rahel became indignant. She had the remaining bottles opened and tasted their contents. At her request, Thaddeus also tasted and admitted that the wine was excellent. He pretended to be gravely disturbed because of his unfounded suspicion of the unreliability of the Berger wares.

He begged Rahel to pardon him and deferentially took her hand, which the chaste girl, whose hand had never before been touched by a stranger, did not withdraw. On the contrary, his gallantry pleased her; she was altogether pleased by the outcome of the entire episode.

In the meantime, the wine had not failed to have its effect. Hour after hour passed, and the conversation between Rahel and the priest became more and more vivacious. Fascinated, she listened to his words; a sinister attraction held her spellbound before him. She was so interested in his words that she did not notice the passage of the hours.

When she finally bethought herself of going home and took her departure she voluntarily extended her hand and Thaddeus pressed it, conscious of victory.

This incident had a devastating effect upon Rahel's temperament. Every word of Thaddeus aroused in her heart a violent storm and a longing for an unknown world. From this time on she felt impelled to exchange confidences with Thaddeus, and he was never out of her thought. Thaddeus now began to order wine almost daily and his servant was the bearer of messages between him and Rahel. In this way she was drawn more and more into the net which Thaddeus had spun for her. She was always in a trance, wandering about in a strange dream world.

* * *

On the street of the Dominicans, on the slope of a hill, ran a long row of luxuriantly leafed trees, leading to a bridge. It was the custom of the inhabitants of Prague in those days to repair to this spot on hot summer days where they would promenade and seek the refreshing coolness of the shade afforded by these trees.

Rahel, too, used occasionally to spend a brief hour after business had closed in this grove where she would walk about for recreation after the day's labor.

One hot July afternoon, Rahel left the store and, seized with a wild impulse, whose origin she could not explain, and did not wish to fathom, she went out toward this promenade.

Slowly and directly she went on her way, not favoring the people she passed with even a look. One would almost have called her haughty, aloof, and heartless.

Her soul became more and more lonely, more and more dismal. Well she knew that the next few hours would open a deep chasm between her and her father's house. But she was already too tightly caught in the meshes of Thaddeus' net to tear herself free. She wished to remain, but her feet carried her along as if she had lost all control over them.

The balmy evening breeze which wafted to her the sweet fragrance of the rustling linden trees, intoxicated her and robbed her of the courage to refrain from taking a mad step. She crossed the bridge. In the street of the Dominicans stood the monastery of Thaddeus. Thither the wild longings of her soul drew her.

Upon reaching the garden wall, she looked about her on every side, hesitated once more, then finally rapped on the gate of the monastery, which after a few moments closed behind her.

It had already been dark a long time. Rahel did not return to her home that night.

* * *

The perplexity of her parents can easily be imagined. The disappearance of Jewish girls was, in those days, no rare occurrence; indeed, it was a frequent event, and the abyss which

112

swallowed up these lost girls was known to all.

In deepest anxiety, the father and the mother of Rahel waited upon Thaddeus and implored him, with heartrending words, to restore their stolen daughter. Thaddeus, however, ardently faithful to his convictions, insisted with well simulated innocence, that he had not even seen Rahel. The parents could do naught but return to their home, their souls filled with anguish, their hearts heavy with the bitterness of failure.

Thaddeus, in the meantime, bethought himself that the authorities, who held Reb Michael Berger in great respect, might take action in his behalf, and he felt that it would be prudent to settle Rahel in a small, separate room, which he furnished with all kinds of comforts and conveniences.

Every morning, he would call upon her to instruct her in the teachings of Christianity. The first few days, Rahel was delighted by the new studies. But one morning, when Thaddeus came to see her, he noticed that a profound change must have come over her; she seemed depressed, sighed deeply, and her beautiful, rosy face was marked by freshly shed tears.

He asked her: "Why are you so sad today, Rahel? Is there some sorrow that weighs upon your heart? Then confide the cause to me."

Rahel answered tearfully that she felt lonely in her seclusion and wished to leave the monastery as soon as possible.

Was she perhaps seized with remorse, with a longing to turn back?

Thaddeus realized that the seclusion had an unfavorable effect on Rahel's spirit, and he decided to seek a fiancé for her, and to have her married immediately after her baptism. He informed Rahel, consolingly, of his intentions, and pictured to her the prospects of soon becoming the mistress of a magnificent castle.

In the environs of Prague, there lived at that time Count Waldberg, an old squire, with whom Thaddeus was on intimately friendly terms. This Count had an only child, a son, Ladislaus by name, who had just completed his studies in Paris.

Thaddeus persuaded the Count to give his son in marriage to Rahel. He extolled her beauty, her education, and her refined personality, but

he emphasized especially the great service which
the Count would be doing for the Holy Church
by taking this neophyte into his family.

Love at First Sight.

The Count and his son were favorably inclined
to consider this proposal and it was arranged that
they should come to Prague the following Sunday,
to make the acquaintance of the girl and, if all
went well, to celebrate the betrothal.

When the Count and his son came to visit him,
Thaddeus prepared a rich banquet in their honor.
Rahel, apprised in advance of the coming of the
guests, had dressed with special care, and the
two men were astounded at her beauty. Ladislaus
fell in love with her at first sight.

The repast lasted almost the entire night and
during the whole time Ladislaus had eyes, ears
and voice only for Rahel, with whose high intelligence he was delighted. He did not take his
gaze from her. In Rahel's heart, too, there welled
up sensations of bliss and her face glowed with
a dreamy longing. After the meal, the engagement
was contracted. It was agreed that in about two

months, Rahel's conversion to Christianity should be consummated and the marriage take place on the same day.

In Rahel's breast was a feeling of rapturous joy. At this moment she felt herself to be far removed from her parents, her race, her religion; indeed, she almost abominated these in her heart. With a rosy picture of a glorious future in her mind's eye, she waited blissfully for the moment when the last tie with them would be sundered forever.

Ladislaus presented her with a costly ring, engraved with his name and the arms of his family, and after tenderly taking leave of his bride, he returned home with his father.

In the meantime the parents of Rahel did not rest in their endeavors to tear their daughter out of Thaddeus' hands. They went to their relative, the renowned Gaon, Rabbi Jacob Guinzburg, the minister of the Jewish congregation of Friedburg, and they implored him with bitter tears to help them in bringing about the rescue of their child.

Rabbi Guinzburg welcomed them most sympathetically, but explained to them that it was not out of indifference toward their plight that

116

he was unable to take any part in the tragic circumstances. After a little reflection he said to them: "In Prague, you know, lives Rabbi Loew, my boyhood friend, and who is better able to help you than he?"

He addressed a letter to Rabbi Loew in which he explained his powerlessness to do anything and begged him in the most urgent terms to help his relatives in their misfortune.

It was already quite late at night when Reb Michael Berger and his wife returned to Prague. Berger went at once to the house of Rabbi Loew, and after he had greeted him most reverently and had been welcomed gently and hospitably by the Rabbi, Reb Michael delivered the letter of the Friedburg minister.

Rabbi Loew Promises Help.

Before he even opened the letter, Rabbi Loew guessed its contents. Had he not already heard of the calamity which had befallen Michael Berger? Reb Michael told him in a most pathetic manner of all the steps which had been taken for the rescue of his daughter, steps which had all been vain, and added that now he had placed all his hopes in Rabbi Loew.

The great Rabbi went over in his mind all the difficulties of the problem before him. It was extremely distasteful to him to come again into opposition with Thaddeus. Finally, however, his heart which always beat with righteousness gained the mastery over his head. He promised to set to work to endeavor to bring about Rahel's release, but he insisted upon the strictest secrecy in order that his steps should not be hampered. Rabbi Loew asked Berger for additional details on various matters; he especially wished to learn whether Berger had any relatives abroad with whom Rahel could live after her release and when he heard that Reb Michael had a brother in Amsterdam he was greatly pleased.

It was not long before Ladislaus also learned of the tragic death of his financee. Grief over her painful death went deep into his heart. Now, indeed, did his love for Rahel flare up in a bright flame, consuming his soul. He renounced, at once, all the joys of life, did not eat, did not drink, and avoided all society. Rahel would not disappear from his heart. And he became melancholy.

His father, Count Waldberg, understood his pain; he also had experienced in his youth a similar tragic love, and he looked about him in the circle of the high nobility for a bride for his son. But no maiden pleased Ladislaus.

Day by day his appearance grew worse. He felt that the only way in which he could heal his wounded soul was to marry another Rahel, a Jewish girl. As he knew, however, that no respectable Jewish girl would marry a non-Jew, even though he be a Count, he decided to go abroad, become converted to Judaism and so achieve his aim.

Not wishing to reveal his secret resolve to his father, he told him that he would forget his unfortunate bride if he went to Venice and, in that world-famed city of beauty and art, resume his studies. With a heavy heart, the old Count gave his consent. The absence of Ladislaus would be a painful trial for him, but he found solace in the hope that his son's stay in Venice would make him again healthy and care-free. Though it was heartbreaking for him to tear himself away from his parental home and his native land, yet Ladislaus took hold of the staff of the wanderer and set out for the land of the unknown.

Ladislaus' destination was Friedburg where the before-mentioned Rabbi Guinzburg was the incumbent of the rabbinical post, and through his extraordinary scholarship was educating hundreds of pupils. Ladislaus sought him out. He told Rabbi Guinzburg of all his past and revealed to him his unshakable decision to become converted to Judaism. With kindly but serious mien, as though he wished to penetrate all the thoughts of the young man, Rabbi Guinzburg listened to him. But true to the words of the sages: "Proselytes are just as harmful to Israel as a plague," he hesitated to induct Ladislaus into the covenant of Israel. When, however, the young man declared to the rabbi that he would not give him any peace until he pitied him, the latter promised to comply with his wish. After explaining to him the duties of a Jew, the Rabbi had Ladislaus inducted into the Abrahamic covenant, and changed his name to Abraham Jeschurun.

The rabbi then arranged for his instruction in Hebrew, and it was not long before he accepted Abraham as a pupil in the Talmud.

As the conversion of a Christian to Judaism was strongly objected to in Germany, Rabbi Jacob, concerned over the fate of Jeschurun, advised him to go to Amsterdam where religious freedom prevailed and where no persecution was to be feared. He gave Jeschurun a letter to the principal of a Talmudical academy in Amsterdam, in which he begged the recipient to receive the bearer, "a relative of mine," hospitably and to give him a place in his school. Rabbi Jacob, in taking leave of Jeschurun blessed him with the wish that he should find in Amsterdam the life-companion whom Heaven had selected for him; and he told him further that he would know it was the right maiden by this sign—that she would be introduced to him as a relative of the Rabbi of Friedburg.

Immediately upon his arrival in Amsterdam Jeschurun waited upon the rector of the Academy and delivered Rabbi Jacob's letter of introduction. He was most cordially welcomed by the principal, who soon came to recognize and admire the ardor and alertness of his new pupil. It was not long before Jeschurun became renowed as a scholar. Besides, his quiet, modest, unaggressive mien won him a way into many hearts and he quickly acquired a large number of friends.

When the second year at the academy came to an end, his master advised Jeschurun to return to his native land and take unto himself a wife, as it was not considered respectable for a man of his years to be single. The young man answered that he preferred to remain in Amsterdam where there were so many scholars, which was not the case in his own home, and that he would like to marry a woman in Amsterdam.

The rector of the school, thereupon told Jeschurun's friends to be on the look-out for a suitable match. One day, someone spoke to Jeschurun about a young woman who was the niece of one Chayim Burger, a wine seller. Among the many qualifications ascribed to her was that she was related to Rabbi Guinzburg of Friedburg. A ray of joy passed over the pale face of Jeschurun, when he heard this. He began to suspect that Rabbi Jacob had sent him to Amsterdam in order that he should meet this girl. Without hesitation, he accepted the proposal and a few days later the bethothal of Jeschurun and Reb Chayim Burger's niece took place.

A few days before the wedding, the groom bought a number of costly ornaments for his bride, among them a beautiful ring set with brilliants. When he asked her to try this on, she drew from her finger an old ring which she laid upon a table. Jeschurun idly picked this up to look at it, and when he saw it he was overcome and fainted.

Brought back to consciousness and asked for the cause of his spell of weakness, Jeschurun implored his bride truthfully to explain to him how she had come into possession of the ring. From her first words, he recognized that before him stood his beloved Rahel, whose image had never left his mind and love for whom had never left his heart. With an exclamation of rapture, he pressed her to his breast and covered her face with kisses.

Shortly thereafter, the wedding of Rahel and Ladislaus, now Jeschurun, was celebrated.

In the same year Count Waldberg, the father of Ladislaus died. Thereupon, Jeschurun took possession of the family estate, and after various necessary changes had been made, a great banquet was arranged, which was attended by the bride's relatives and a large number of friends. Rabbi Loew also received an invitation and a splendid equipage was sent to bring him to the castle. He came, accompanied by the Golem.

It was at this joyous banquet that the secret of Rahel's miraculous release from the monastery was revealed. As Thaddeus had, in the meantime, been caught red-handed in a criminal attempt to bring disaster upon the Jews of Prague and had been sentenced to imprisonment, Rabbi Loew did not fear to do this.

Jeschurun gave over to Rabbi Loew a large sum of money to be distributed among philanthropic institutions, and when, some years later, his wife's parents passed to the Beyond, he presented their estate to the community, and he endowed their house as a *Beth Hamidrash,* which was thereafter known by his name.

GAUGHT IN HIS OWN NET

IN the year 5345 (1585) on the evening of the 13th day of Nisan, Rabbi Loew, having cleaned away all leavened food in preparation for the *Passover*, was reading by the light of a taper, from the prayer book the formula *Kol chamira*. Suddenly the light, which was being held by the sexton Abraham Chayim, was extinguished and Rabbi Loew was unable to complete the prayer, for he made it an invariable practice to recite prayers from the book and not from memory. He used to say that he could tell from the characters what was the mood of Heaven, whether mercy or severity,—if the latter, he understood how to temper it. He motioned to the servant to relight the taper, but it was again extinguished; and this mysterious happening occurred again and again.

Rabbi Loew was frightened and commanded the terrified sexton to light the wall lamps and to read the prayer to him. The latter did so, but instead of reading *"Kol chamiro vachamio de-iko birschusi"* (all leaven which is in my possession) he read *"Kol chamira vachamia de-ika be-chumeschi"* (all leaven which is in *the fifth.*)

"What's that?" cried Rabbi Loew, alarmed at the error.

The sexton was startled but he read the passage again in the same way.

Rabbi Loew became deathly pale. Wiping the sweat on his forehead he said: "Now I grasp it all. A misfortune threatens us—they wish to extinguish our light. The same thing was conveyed in my dream on the night of *Shabbas Ha-Gadol"* (the great Sabbath, preceding Passover).

The Dream.

He commanded all the people to go home, and there remained with him only his son-in-law Rabbi Yitzchak and the two attendants, Abraham Chayim and Joseph Golem, to whom Rabbi Loew spoke as follows:

"Last Sabbath night I saw in a dream a fire blazing from the *Funfer Palast,* which sprang

126

across the street to the Altneu Synagogue which was filled with worshippers. As I ascribed no significance to this dream, the danger which threatens us was revealed to me by Heaven. Now I understand the meaning: in *Funfer Palast* lies some *chometz,* something leaven, which has been smuggled in in order to start a blood accusation against the Jews of Prague. Our enemies mean in this way to extinguish the Jewish light. We must at once go to the *Funfer Palast,* seek for the *chometz* and get rid of it at once."

Rabbi Loew was full of concern,—a concern which became deeper when he recalled that a few days before a child of Wachlaw, a monastery attendant, had mysteriously disappeared.

The *Funfer Palast* was so called because this building was situated where five streets converged. Its architecture indicated that it had been built in the remote past, during the time that paganism still flourished in Prague, for it had all the characteristics of a shrine of the Sun-god. The Palace was government property, and three sides of it were masses of ruins. According to tradition, many years before, an eccentric monarch had lived in it, who never allowed himself to be seen, and who had built a subterranean passage from the palace to the so called "green" monastery. This was the seat of the Jew hating monk, Thaddeus. The Altneu Synagogue was opposite the Palace. All sorts of tales were current about this sinister ruin to the effect that it was haunted by evil spirits. No one passed it without shuddering.

Thither went Rabbi Loew and his companion while the city was enveloped in the silence and darkness of midnight. A rainy damp air blew in their faces. The building which they were approaching was black, and bore traces of many years of neglect. The pillars of the court in the endless rows, as they emerged from the darkness in the light of torches, and again disappeared, aroused weird feelings.

Rabbi Loew was not a little anxious as he ascended the worm eaten, broken wooden staircase with its seemingly interminable steps. His attendant Abraham Chayim was also fearful, but Joseph Golem remained calm and carefree. With burning *Havdalah* tapers they entered the house, with its doorless and windowless openings. The roof also had partly collapsed, so that the cloud covered sky looked down into the dreary ruins.

Odor of the Tomb.

After casting a glance about, Rabbi Loew turned his steps toward the cellar. The odor of the tomb permeated the place and a plaintive whining was audible. The Rabbi listened and caught the sound distinctly. It sounded now like the whimpering of a child, now like the whining of a dog, now it would rise in volume until it finally resembled the roaring of a lion.

As Rabbi Loew and his sexton entered the cellar, they recited three times the psalm beginning "O thou that dwellest in the covert of the Most High" (Ps. 91), at which the whining, whimpering, and roaring ceased at once. As they went forward, however, stones began to fall down upon them.

Then Rabbi Loew said to the Golem: "Do thou, Joseph, go thyself within and look most carefully about. If you find anything at all that would lead to the suspicion of a murder, bring it here to me at once. I shall await thee!"

With the burning taper in his hand, the Golem entered the cellar region, and it was not long before he returned with two little baskets, covered over with cloths. Rabbi Loew uncovered these in turn. In the first was found a dead child wrapped in a *tallith* (praying shawl); in the other were thirty small phials containing a red fluid, which Rabbi Loew quickly ascertained was blood. On the phials were labels bearing the names of members of the Jewish community, including Rabbi Loew, his son, his son-in-law, and other outstanding individuals. Rabbi Loew was overjoyed to have come upon so perilous a "treasure trove". He ordered the Golem to carry the basket containing the body of the child through the subterranean passage into the cellar of Thaddeus the monk, to place it there among the barrels of wine, and to return at once.

When the Golem came back about a half hour later, Rabbi Loew told him to secure a spade and dig a deep hole, into which the vials of blood were cast, the hole then being filled in and covered.

On the morning of the day before *Passover*, at about ten o'clock, there suddenly appeared in the Jewish quarter, a large number of gendarmes led by the chief of Police. They scattered and began a painstaking search of all the houses. The chief himself, accompanied by Thaddeus, undertook the search of Rabbi Loew's house, and of those of his children and the community officials.

Search Fruitless.

Their search proving fruitless, the police departed. But as they passed the *Funfer Palast*, Thaddeus remarked, with studied carelessness, that it might be well to look into the cellar of this ruin, in view of its proximity to the synagogue. The chief of police acted upon this suggestion. The entire cellar was searched, but not a trace was found of what Thaddeus was sure would be discovered, and he became pale with chagrin and disappointment.

During these unexpected happenings, the Jews were dreadfully worried and they came, trembling with fear, to Rabbi Loew, who quieted them, saying: "Be comforted, brothers! God's help will come in due season and will guard you ever."

At the approach of Easter, Thaddeus ordered his servant Wachlaw to take an inventory of the wine on hand in order to ascertain how much more was needed for the holidays. While Wachlaw was engaged in this occupation, he came upon the corpse of a child. Upon examining it, he was horror stricken and almost swooned, for he recognized his missing child. Without a moment's delay he hastened to the prefecture and reported the matter to the police. A commision of inquiry was at once dispatched to the spot and their investigation proved that Thaddeus had slain the child. His motive was two fold. First, he wished to raise a blood accusation against the Jews; and second, he wished to punish Wachlaw, who, he believed, had delivered Rahel Berger to her parents. [See a previous episode in this series, *The Romance of Rahel and Ladislaus.*] When the child disappeared, Thaddeus persuaded its parents that in view of the approach of the Jewish *Passover,* their child had undoubtedly been slaughtered by the Jews so that his blood might be used in their ritual. It was upon this suggestion that the parents had gone to the authorities and insisted upon the search of the Jewish quarter.

At first, Thaddeus denied his wicked deed, but when he saw that this was useless because an entire chain of circumstances pointed to him as the guilty man, he made a clean breast of the matter, brazenly justifying his gruesome crime

132

by saying that he desired to revenge himself on his servant because he helped the Jews to release a girl from his grasp. This charge Wachlaw stoutly denied, insisting that the girl had taken her own life because Thaddeus had imprisoned her.

The monk was sentenced to ten years imprisonment and was unfrocked as one unworthy to continue in his sacred office. May a similar fate overtake all Thine enemies, O Lord!

Who had cleaned out from the *Funfer Palast* the *chometz* which might have soured the lives of the Jews of Prague, only Rabbi Loew and his confidents knew.

THE GOLEM FETCHES FISH
AND APPLES

RABBI Loew's wife, Pearl, had once had a disagreeable remembrance from the Golem, as we have told before, when she made use of his services for secular purposes.

Several years had gone by, and she had quite forgotten that incident, when she wanted to marry off a poor orphan girl. She and Rabbi Loew took the place of bridal parents, furnished the dowry, provided the trousseau and prepared a great wedding feast, to which they invited the most distinguished people of the community.

Pearl and her servants were entirely occupied with the preparations, so she had the fish and apples for the wedding brought by the Golem.

Was she not engaged in performing a great deed, a *mitzvah*, to marry off a poor girl? So she assumed that this use of the Golem would not be considered as a private service.

134

She said to the Golem: "Go to the Moldau and bring from the fisherman the live fish which have been ordered. When you have returned with the fish, hasten to the fruit market and bring a pail of nice apples."

Thereupon she gave him two strips of paper. They were notes, one to the fisherman and one to the fruitvender, instructing them to deliver the ordered articles to the Golem.

The Golem went to the Moldau and got a live carp weighing 20 pounds. In his haste, he did not wait for a bag, but he attempted to manage the situation in another way, by putting the fish in the bosom of his blouse which was fastened with a heavy belt. He placed it in such a way that the head of the fish was turned downward, while the largest part with the tail protruded from the top.

On the way home, the fish gave the Golem so violent a slap in the face with its tail that he was shaken off his feet.

The Golem could not forgive the fish that slap. He went, full speed, right back to the Moldau and threw the fish into the water with such tremendous force that it sank to the bottom. He did it so quickly that the fishermen could not stop him.

He returned home with empty hands.

When Pearl asked him about the fish, he told, through motions with the hands and facial grimaces, what had happened to him, and how, in order to punish the fish, he had thrown it into the water.

Everybody laughed heartily; Pearl, however, was despondent, for, in the meantime, the hour for fishmarketing had passed, and the wedding remained without fish.

Nor did the apple incident end very happily.

Pearl had already forgotten that she had also sent the Golem on that errand, but he had already gone to the fruit market and delivered to the fruit-vender the note of his mistress.

She weighed out the required quantity and wanted to have him take the apples with him in a bag.

He indicated, however, that he was able to take the whole stock of apples on his shoulders. When the fruit-woman laughed at him he flew into a rage.

Quick as a flash, he took the woman, together

with her stand and her baskets filled with fruit, upon his shoulders, and carried her, to the astonishment of all, through the city, with the swiftness of the wind.

The woman, frightened to death, screamed with all her might, but in vain. No one could even attempt to deliver her from the situation.

When he arrived in the court-yard of Rabbi Loew, the Golem unloaded his burden, ran quickly into the kitchen, and called out Pearl, with signs and gestures.

In the meantime a great number of people came rushing in, curious to know what was to be the fate of the fruit-vendor.

With great swiftness, the Golem put the fruit-stand together the same way as it had stood in the market, the crowd watching the performance.

He lifted the fruit-vendor and carried her over to the stand.

Through his window Rabbi Loew saw a large crowd of people gathered in the yard. He came out, and when he saw the Golem in the midst of the crowd, he understood that the people were again gazing at a Golem spectacle.

He called: "Joseph, come to me!"

The Golem left everything in the place as it was and hastened to the Rabbi, to whom he related, through gestures, the case.

On Rabbi Loew's face there was seen a suppressed smile.

Turning to his wife, he said:

"You have made here today another wedding. But from now on you will know how to regard my word, not to employ the Golem for your errands!"

Since then it is said even to this day in Prague, when one speaks of something that is not right, that is topsy-turvy: "It is like the story of the Golem with the fish;" and when a fruit-vendor gets into an argument with a customer, she says: "Are you perhaps the Golem of the great Rabbi Loew?"

STORY OF TWO BERELS

DURING the lifetime of Rabbi Loew there lived in Prague a teacher who was called in the ghetto "Jacob the Great." With him, two poor orphan youths who had immigrated from Roumania, found employment as assistants in the *heder*.

Both assistants were named Berel; one of them was of reddish complexion and auburn hair, the other was dark, and so they were called, according to their outward appearance, respectively, "Berel the Red," and "Berel the Black."

The two Berels were close friends and lived intimate, brotherly lives. Their employer, Jacob the Great, was very well satisfied with them, as were also all the people whose children they brought to and from the *heder*. They, therefore, received many presents and succeeded in amassing a little capital. Both were married at almost the same time, securing wives from respectable middle-class houses, and they thereupon decided to open up a butcher shop in partnership. Little by little this enterprise prospered, and they began to trade cattle in which they had luck also. It was not long before they were known as "the rich Berels" in Prague and environs. In time they bought a large stone house in which they both lived and they got along together just as satisfactorily as they did in those days when, two penniless youngsters, they had come to Prague. Their manner of living was the same in every particular as neither of them wished to outdo the other by a single *kreutzer.*

And yet, in one regard, they were not alike.

Berel the Red was sourrounded by a crowd of beautiful children, sons and daughters, and the Angel of Death had not crossed his threshold, as if he did not know that there was a Red Berel in Prague who had many children. Black Berel, on the other hand, had only daughters and ugly ones at that, and the Angel of Death was a frequent guest in his house. In despite of this, however, the two wives of the Berels lived peacefully with one another. Indeed, the wife of Black Berel could not help inwardly envying her friend; but as she was a prudent and good woman she

140

did not permit this envy to come to the surface.

But the midwife Esther, who in all Jewish houses not only practiced her profession but was also a confidant, a friend of the family, who knew all the joys and sorrows, pitied in her heart the unfortunate mother, the wife of Black Berel.

It happened that both women found themselves in a blessed condition at the same time. While the wife of Berel the Red looked forward to the fateful hour with joy, expecting to present her husband with another healthy infant, the wife of Berel the Black awaited this hour with anxiety. Esther was sorry for her and made a plan to heal the sick heart of this unfortunate woman.

As accident would have it, both women were confined in one and the same night and both had male children born to them,—the wife of Red Berel hat a strong one, while the wife of Black Berel brought a weak puny little boy into the world. Esther immediately carried out her plan with great skill; she exchanged the two children without the mothers being aware of it. This time there was a feast of joy in the house of Black Berel,—the circumcision of a son, a splendid little fellow at that.

Years passed. Esther, the midwife, died. The children whom she had exchanged for one another grew up and became the favorites of their parents. Then came the time when Black Berel began to think of the marriage of his son. When he disclosed this desire to his friend, Berel the Red, the latter proposed to give him his daughter as wife for his son; this offer was accepted with joy and the betrothal soon took place.

A year later Rabbi Loew was called to perform the marriage ceremony. Then something singular occurred. As Rabbi Loew, standing under the marriage canopy in the court of the Altneu synagogue, took the wineglass in his hand in order to recite the first blessing, the glass fell out of his hand and the wine was spilled. Another glass of wine was handed to him and he began to recite: "Blessed art Thou . . ." but he was not able to say the word "Eternal," began to tremble, and the glass again fell to the ground.

Rabbi Loew was frightened. All the wedding guests were startled. In the meantime, the sexton, Abraham Chayim had noticed that the wine flask was empty and he beckoned to the Golem

to get a full flask out of the cellar of the Rabbi.
The Golem hurried to the house of Rabbi Loew
on the opposite side of the street but when he
came to the door he stopped suddenly. The people
called to him to hurry to bring the wine. And yet
the Golem did not go into the cellar but into the
Rabbi's office and there wrote something on
a card. Then instead of bringing wine he
approached Rabbi Loew and, drawing this card
from his pocket, handed it to him. Upon looking
at it, Rabbi Loew became as pale as a corpse and
groaned. All the people were astounded at this;
they understood at once that there was something
peculiar going on. Then the community heard
the Rabbi ask the Golem: "Who told you this?"
And the Golem stepped through the crowd,
beckoning Rabbi Loew to follow, and pointed
to the window of the synagogue as if he wished
to say: "There is the person who told me it."
Rabbi Loew gazed for a few minutes at the window and returned to the assemblage. Standing
again under the canopy he said: "The marriage
cannot take place today, for I must first make a
thorough investigation."

On the same day, after midnight, Rabbi Loew

called the Golem into his study, gave him a whispered command and handed over to him his staff. The Golem left at once, went out of the city, and returned in about an hour.

On the following morning, Rabbi Loew gave instructions that seats be prepared for him and his two colleagues in the southeastern corner of the synagogue, and that, several yards further to the south, a screen of the height of a man be erected. Then he announced that those persons who would attend synagogue on that day were not to go home after prayers but were to remain and to stand up on the west side of the *almemor* (reading desk).

When Rabbi Loew ended the prayers, he sat down at a table with his two colleagues; the three wore their prayer shawls and their phylacteries. Then Rabbi Loew sent the sexton Abraham Chayim to fetch the two Berels, together with their wives and children, including the bridegroom and the bride. When these appeared he had them seated at a table on the north side, and demanded that they should relate all the experiences they had passed through since their marriage. The two Berels and their wives took

144

turns to describe their lives. In the course of their recital Black Berel and his wife told many a sad tale.

Then Rabbi Loew sent for the Golem, gave him his staff and commanded him in the presence of the entire community: "Go to the cemetery and call the soul of the midwife Esther here so that she may make a disposition." After the Rabbi had handed to him a small piece of paper, Joseph Golem left the synagogue.

After about a half hour he returned, stepped up to Rabbi Loew, handed back the staff, pointed with his hand toward the screen and made it understood that he had obeyed the command to summon the soul of the midwife. A deathly silence reigned; the assemblage was mute with terror.

Rabbi Loew spoke to the dead: "We, the leaders of this court of justice, command thee, Esther, to tell us clearly and distinctly how it happens that this bridal pair are brother and sister."

And the dead told the story as we have already related it. Those present who were standing on the west side of the Almenor heard only an indistinct murmur. The rabbinical company, however, and the bridal pair and their parents heard every word clearly. Concluding, the dead said in a voice of lamentation: "It is twelve years now since I departed from this world and to this very day my soul can find no peace unless I make good this sin which I committed. Rabbi Loew is to be thanked that I have been permitted to be present at a marriage between a brother and a sister and to prevent it. Had the marriage taken place my soul would never have found rest. I beg the Rabbis to have mercy on my soul and to arrange that the sons of the two Berels should again be exchanged. If the statement of one who is dead is not regarded as creditible, then I produce another proof from the time of my life on earth,— let my diary be examined; it is in the keeping of my daughter; and there will be found my notes about the exchange of the children . . ."

A sorrowful weeping was then heard and all those present wept in sympathy.

There was a pause during which Rabbi Loew ordered the sexton to bring from the daughter of the midwife all the papers of her mother, and Rabbi Loew found the notes of the dead giving the exact date of the occurrence. Then followed a consultation among the rabbis. It was decided that the dead should ask the pardon of the bridegroom and the bride for the offense which she had committed against them, and that if these would pardon her then she would be forgiven. Then her voice was heard saying: "I, Esther, who brought you into the world, ask your forgiveness!"

"We forgive thee!" answered the bridegroom and the bride with trembling lips.

Then Rabbi Loew and the assessors arose and said: "We, members of the court of justice, declare thee, Esther, free of all punishment and therefore the heavenly judge will also declare thee free. And now go in peace, rest in peace until the eternal awakes all the dead at the time of resurrection!"

Then Rabbi Loew ordered the screen to be removed as a sign that the dead was no longer present. He turned to the assembled community and said: "The matter is clear, that the two youngest sons of the two Berels were exchanged by the midwife, Esther. Thus, the bridegroom is really the son of the Red Berel, that is, a brother of the bride. I, therefore, declare this betrothal annulled. It would, however, be right if now the proper son of the Black Berel marry the bride who until now he had supposed to be his sister."

The two Berels at once declared themselves willing that this should be so and Rabbi Loew wrote the new betrothal contract. He called for the community's memorial book and wrote in it an account of this wonderful occurrence so that future generations would know of it, and he confirmed it with his own signature and with those of his rabbinical colleagues.

THE DROPPED TORAH SCROLL

I T happened once on the Day of Atonement of
the year 5347 (1587) that in the Synagogue
where Rabbi Loew was holding services, a
member of the community dropped the Torah
Scroll as he lifted it after the afternoon prayers,
in order to replace it into the Ark of the Law.

The incident caused all the members of the
congregation great fear, for such an occurrence
was considered, from days of yore, a bad omen.

Rabbi Loew, too, was troubled, and so he
proclaimed the day of the 13th of Tishri a fast
for all the community members praying in that
Synagogue.

That day the Rabbi sent up a dream-question,
asking what sin it was that had brought about
that unfortunate occurrence. He did not, however, get any clear answer, but a response in
these letters: *Aleph-aleph-ayin lamed-taw-shin
lamed-lamed-vov.*

Rabbi Loew could not make out what the interpretation was. So he wrote the characters on a piece of paper, which he gave to the Golem, with instructions to find an explanation of those letters.

As soon as the Golem looked at the words, he took down a prayer-book from the book-shelf, opened it, and pointed to the chapter of the Torah which is read during the afternoon service on the Day of Atonement. The letters, revealed to Rabbi Loew, were an abbreviation of the verse reading, "And thou shalt not lie carnally with thy neighbor's wife, to defile thyself with her." (Lev. xviii, 20.)

Rabbi Loew knew then that the man who dropped the Torah had committed adultery, and that it was because of this sin that the Torah had fallen from his hands. He sent for the man, and told him, confidentially, of what he had learned. Weeping, the man confessed his sin, and he begged the Rabbi to impose a penance on him.

Rabbi Loew went still further. He brought about a divorce between the adulterous woman and her husband, in accordance with the laws of Moses and the Rabbis.

THE RUIN

A FEW miles outside of Prague there was a deserted, empty structure, called by the people "The Ruin" for short. Years before, this building had served as a powder mill. Rumors were afoot among the country folks, Jews as well as Gentiles, that the ruin was haunted by all sorts of ghosts and evil spirits. Some said that at nights they heard music of a large band coming from it; others, again, that they had seen whole packs of black dogs near it. The ruin and its environs were, therefore, the dread of all passers-by. One man once swore that one night as he was passing by the ruin, he saw a soldier standing on top of the roof and blowing a trumpet.

One day, it happened that a Prague Jew, on his way home from the village, was followed by a large dog, who finally disappeared in the ruin. The man was terribly frightened, and reached home almost unconscious. He told his family of his experience. That night, his family heard the man in his sleep bark like a dog, and when they woke him up, he was all covered with beads of perspiration and was so exhausted that he could barely stir. He told them that he dreamt he was riding, like a number of soldiers who were with him, on the back of a black dog, and when the dogs began to bark, the soldiers forced him, too, to bark with them.

His family did not pay much attention to the dream, and persuaded him also that it was only the result of his troubled imagination.

But the man could find no peace. Night after night he was tortured by the same dream. Little by little he lost his strength and as he could not get the needed rest for his work, his business, too, was affected.

Finally he went to Rabbi Loew, accompanied by his family. The man related to the Rabbi the whole story from the beginning and, with tears in his eyes, appealed for counsel and aid.

Rabbi Loew had the man first of all examine his *talis katan* (small prayer shawl) to see whether it was in proper condition, in accordance with the written law. The man found that on one corner two fringes were torn off. The Rabbi then asked him to examine the phylacteries, and he found that those, too, were imperfect. Thereupon Rabbi Loew said: "Now it is clear why you have been pursued and the guardian angels did not protect you." He advised the man to repair the threads and the phylacteries and to take a ritual bath. Then he gave him an amulet with the inscription: "But against any of the children of Israel shall not a dog whet his tongue," (Exodus ix, 1) and he ordered him to bind this amulet around his forehead every night before going to bed. He further ordered the man to change beds with the Golem for seven nights in succession: he was to sleep in the Rabbi's house in the Golem's bed, while the Golem was to sleep in the man's bed at his home.

On the seventh night Rabbi Loew had the Golem secretly come home, gave him his staff and commanded him to go to the ruin after midnight with two large bundles of straw and to set it on fire, so that it be burned to ashes.

On the seventh day Rabbi Loew told the man that he could go home in peace.

The following morning the passers-by saw that the ruin had disappeared leaving no trace behind. Since then, the "ruin" ceased to be the fear of the neighborhood.

COUNT
JACOB BARTHOLOMEW

IN a village, several miles from Prague, lived a
Count by the name of Bartholomew, possessor
of ten villages. He had an only son, Oscar, an
educated youth, who was the very apple of
his eye.

In the villages of the Count there lived many
Jews, who were all making a good living as lessees
of the estates and the inns, and as rent farmers.
The Count and his son were friendly disposed
toward them, and this was the traditional attitude.

When the Count became a widower, he made
it his practice, in order to forget his grief, to visit
his Jews on Saturdays and Jewish holidays. At
one house he would eat fish, at another *kugel*,
and so on. Frequently he would bring his son
along.

In the village in which the Count had his
summer residence lived a Jew who had been

overseer of the estate for many years. His great-grandfather, Reb Moses, after whom he was named, had lived in this village and was steward to the grandfather of Count Bartholomew. This Jew had an only child, a daughter, who was just about the age of the Count's son. This young man upon meeting Rosa at the house of the overseer, fell ardently in love with her. He confided the fact to his father and implored him to let him marry the girl.

So, once when the Count was sitting, on the Sabbath, at the table of his overseer, with a flagon of good wine before him, he said to the Jew:

"Moses, if your Rosa is willing to become a Christian, my son would marry her, and I would make you a present of the income from the estate."

Moses was downcast. Of course he did not permit himself to see in the Count's suggestion any threat, yet he looked at the landowner as a deer at its hunter, and, thinking to find a way out, he said:

"How can Your Highness think for a moment of marrying the young Count, the scion of one of the noblest families of Bohemia, with whom many titled ladies would be glad to unite—how can you think of marrying him to a plain Jewish girl?"

"I consider the lineage of a Jew no less noble than that of a Count," answered Bartholomew with a smile.

Rosa Marries Isaac.

Moses understood that the matter was not an ordinary one and, hearkening to the advice of good friends, he hastened to bring about Rosa's marriage. A poor, orphaned youth, of a good Prague family, became her husband. His name was Isaac the Levite. About a year later, Rosa gave birth to a son who was named Jacob.

When this boy was about two years old, a dreadful plague broke out in Prague and its environs, and raged for a long time. Thousands were laid low, thousands fled to other regions. Among the former were the overseer Moses, his wife, and their son-in-law, Isaac, the Levite. Rosa and her son came out of the dreadful visitation unscathed.

There were no Jews near by to give the three victims of the plague the burial required by Jewish tradition. The holy society but recently

157

founded by Rabbi Loew in Prague had enough occasion for performing its melancholy duty in its own community; besides they did not know of these deaths. Rosa feared to remain with the corpses. She left the house and wandered aimlessly about with her child. From that moment she was never seen again in those parts.

In Prague and vicinity, it was assumed that the entire family of the overseer had been stricken by the plague. This belief arose from the fact that the Count, upon learning that the dead had been left unburied, considered it advisable to have the house burned down. The news of this aroused deep sorrow in Prague. Many poor people mourned, for Moses had been extremely charitable and no wanderer had ever knocked at his door who had not been hospitably received, in accordance with Jewish tradition.

Just about that time the Count's son Oscar went to Venice on a pleasure trip. It was not long before the Count announced that his son had married the young widow of a Roman diplomat and that the couple would come home in about a year. The widow's son by her first marriage would remain in Venice to complete his education. The couple came home in due time, and the Count's neighbors and tenants were lavish in their praise of the grace, the beauty, and the charm of Oscar's wife.

The Old Count Dies.

Not long thereafter, the old Count died and his son inherited the estate. Then the step-son was brought from Venice and the Count had him registered as his own son, giving his name as Jacob Bartholomew. The married couple loved one another dearly, and they lived very happily together.

When Jacob came of age he married the daughter of a general who had won many laurels; the two daughters who had been born to the Countess were united to Polish noblemen. Ten years later, the Count fell ill and went the way of all flesh.

When Jacob became possessor of his foster-father's estate, he surprised everyone by his attitude of bitter animosity toward Jews. He began to oppress those on his estates, increasing their rents and restricting the rights they had enjoyed for generations. Finally, he decided to rid his estates entirely of Jews. This decision fell upon more than a hundred Jewish families, about eight hundred souls, like a thunderbolt.

When they received the dire report, almost all of them went to the castle to implore him to relent, or, at least, to give them a little more time to arrange their affairs. But they were not even admitted. In their perplexity, they repaired to Prague and called upon Rabbi Loew. The latter comforted them by saying that the Eternal, as in every great crisis, would help them in this one, and he asked them to return a week later.

That night when Rabbi Loew was asleep, he dreamed that a man appeared before him and made this statement:

"I am the father of the young Count Jacob Bartholomew. My name is Isaac, son of Aaron the Levite, of Prague, and I was the husband of Rosa, daughter of Moses, the overseer of the estate on which my son is now residing as Count. And when I died at the time of the plague my bewildered wife knew not whither to turn. In desperation she sought shelter at the castle of Count Bartholomew. When the Count and his son were informed of this by a servant, they pitied her and treated her with great tenderness and consideration, giving her and our son a comfortable apartment and supplying her every want. Rosa gradually became accustomed to her life in the castle, forgot her parents and her husband and lived again as before her marriage. She dressed as if her heart had been untouched by grief. His old love for her again flamed in the heart of the young Count. Day after day he became more and more intimate with her, until they reached the decision to marry. Was it her hopeless condition or the leanings of her heart which brought Rosa to this point? Perhaps both. But she firmly refused to become converted to Christianity.

"As the young Count did not wish to arouse any gossip in the neighborhood by marrying a Jewess, he went with Rosa and her child to Venice. There the child was placed in a school, and Oscar married my widow. In order to prevent him from returning to Judaism, the Count purposely hired anti-Semitic tutors and teachers. Since my son has dealt wickedly toward Jews, whose prayers storm the mercy seat, my soul can find no rest. I am driven from the other world into this lower one, because through my son I am to blame for the evils visited upon these Jews. Thrice have I appeared in dreams to my son, revealed to him the fact that he is a Jew, and implored him to leave the Jews in peace. But my son fails to understand the meaning of these dreams, and I am therefore doomed to wander outside the sphere of bliss. I pray thee, therefore, holy man, to have pity on my soul and help it to find rest!" Having completed this recital, the dream image faded.

When Rabbi Loew awoke, he was deeply disturbed by this extraordinary dream. He made inquiries, and confirmed the fact that the overseer Moses actually had a daughter by the name of Rosa; now he remembered the occasion when the man came to him for advice when the Count was pressing him to give his daughter in marriage to Oscar.

On the following Sunday, Rabbi Loew provided the Golem with an amulet which rendered him invisible, and gave him a letter with instructions to deliver it to Count Bartholomew on his drive to church in Prague. That day as the Count was proceeding to church in his barouche, a sealed

162

letter was placed in his hands by an invisible agent. He opened it hastily and read:

"My dear son Jacob: I come from Heaven to tell thee that I, Isaac ben Aaron Halevi of Prague, am thy real father. I am the first husband of thy mother, who is the daughter of Mosca, who in his day was the overseer of thy estate. I and thy mother's parents died during the plague. It was I who gave thee the name Jacob. Now, I pray thee do no evil to the Jews who have lived and earned their bread on thy estates; leave them in peace. Verily I have implored thee in dreams to refrain from evil, but thou wouldst not understand and I must needs come from Heaven to hand thee this message. Since thou hast been oppressing the Jews, my soul finds no peace. Thou needst but ask thy mother and she will reveal to thee the truth about thy parentage. Seek advice and counsel also of the Rabbi of Prague."

To Which People.

Having received this astonishing letter in so mysterious a manner, Count Jacob did not doubt for a moment that it was in fact handed to him by the spirit of his dead father. He returned home, called his mother into a private room and showed her the letter. Bursting into tears, the mother confessed everything and confirmed the letter in every detail.

The young man was bewildered, and said to his mother in a bitter tone: "I was born a Jew and reared as a Christian. Now I do not know to which people to belong!"

The next day he despatched a letter to Rabbi Loew, begging him to come as he wished to consult him on weighty matters. Rabbi Loew remained at the castle a day and a night. What the two spoke about has never been revealed, for the Rabbi never confided this secret to anyone, taking it with him to his grave. What did become known was this, that on the following day the Count cancelled the order expelling the Jews from his estates and, as compensation for the pain and anguish he had caused them, remitted the rents for an entire year. Since that day, he was always a considerate master.

At about the same time, Rabbi Loew had built in Prague a Talmud Torah which he named "Jacob's House." It was said that Count Jacob Bartholomew had given him a handsome sum as a maintenance fund for this school, wishing in this way to preserve his name among his people.

When the Count died he was buried beside his mother in his own garden. This grave of mother and son may still be seen by those who visit S——, a picturesque little village near Prague, where the ivycovered ruins of an old stone castle are still to be seen.

AN ATTAK ON THE GOLEM

AS all know, there were a number of Jewish families from Spain and refugees from Italy, who had come to Prague and settled there. In the course of time, many had met again the members of their families from whom they had been separated amid heartrending cries of woe.

Even before Rabbi Loew came to Prague, it happened once that in one of those families a brother had married his own sister. Only years afterwards—the couple had already been blessed with several children—the close relationship was revealed, through a hereditary wart concealed on a part of the body.

Rabbi Loew and his Rabbinical Council held a consultation at once, when the case was brought to his knowledge, and that same day the legal separation of the couple was effected.

Although Rabbi Loew had it announced that there was no blame attached to the couple and

166

that their marriage was a decree of fate, which it is beyond the power of man to control, and in spite of the fact the family was one of the foremost in Prague and was related to the most distinguished native Prague Jewish families, still there remained a blot on the couple. Their honorable name "Nadler" was converted into a nickname, and the word "wart", in vulgar tongue of the time, came to be designated by the word "Nadler".

This abusive word spread over all Prague, so that when one wished to insult another, he called him „Nadler". Rabbi Loew was enraged when he became aware that that demoralizing abusive word was being circulated, because, on one hand, the blameless family was being deeply offended, and, on the other hand, it had a very harmful effect on the morals of the children, as the nickname penetrated even the children's school.

After preliminary exchange of opinion in writing with the greatest Rabbinical authorities, Rabbi Loew, together with his Rabbinical Council, had, at the blow of a horn and in the presence of two burning black candles, pronounced a ban against any one who would use the word "Nadler" as a nickname or epithet. The ban had its effect, and people took care not to use the word any more.

Still there were in Prague some people who disregarded the prohibition, and who, as formerly, in cases of insults in controversy, would resort to the word "Nadler". Rabbi Loew said of them that they were possessed by the spirit of Korah. (Numbers xvii, 1.)

When Rabbi Loew was informed of this, he sent his servant Abraham Chayim to the leader of those people, a porter, to serve a summons on him to appear before the Rabbinate. But the man retorted boldly: "I will come when I am at leisure." Rabbi Loew became very angry when he heard this. He had Joseph Golem come to him and he ordered him to bring the porter to the Rabbi's house. The Golem betook himself straightway to the house of the porter, grasped him by the back of his neck, and carried him, like a slaughtered little lamb, through the city to Rabbi Loew's house. The latter had gotten a few strong men ready, to administer the lashing due to the perverse fellow. After the punishment was administered, the man had to appear before Rabbi Loew, barefoot, to ask his forgiveness, and to make a vow from then on never to use the word "Nadler".

The porter swore vengeance against the people who had administered the blows to him. His anger was directed in particular against the Golem, and he made up his mind to get even with him.

When the man returned home, he held counsel with his friends as to attacking the Golem and killing him. A favorable opportunity soon presented itself for them to that end.

It was a custom with Rabbi Loew to have fresh cold water brought to him from a neighboring very deep well every week at the close of the Sabbath. When, on the following Saturday evening, the Golem, as usual, appeared at the well and, in order to pull up the water, lowered the wellbucket with the long wooden wellpole, these men fell upon him from behind seized him, and, before he could ward off their grasp, threw him, head down, into the well.

It was a freezing, cold night. If the Golem had been an ordinary human, he would have met death instantly. But to him it did not mean very much. He dived several times in the icecold water and attempted to climb up on the walls. But the men threw stones into the well, inflicting wounds on his nose and his right eye, after which they ran away. The Golem, who was not able to climb upon the smooth walls, swam back and forth and stayed on the surface of the water.

In the meantime, at the house of Rabbi Loew, the people were waiting for the Golem to return. As a few hours passed by, and he had not yet returned, Rabbi Loew sent the old servant Abraham Chayim, who accompanied by two other men, betook himself to the well with a lantern in his hands. When the Golem saw the light of the lantern, he began to clap with his hands. Quickly they lowered the wooden well-pole with the bucket, the Golem stepped into it and was thus pulled up. Bleeding and exhausted, he was led to Rabbi Loew, who ordered that the Golem be undressed and placed near the warm stove. Only on Tuesday, the Golem appeared again before Rabbi Loew, who, through signs, questioned him about his experience. The Golem wrote the answer on paper, and at once asked

170

permission to take revenge on the man who had attempted to kill him. But Rabbi Loew did not grant permission, and said: "The culprits will receive their punishment from Heaven." And so it was. For, all at once, there was formed on the hand of the porter a black wart. It was removed by surgical operation, but it grew back immediately. Then the carrier saw that that was imposed upon him as a punishment of God, because he did not regard the ban of Rabbi Loew. He sent his wife and child to Rabbi Loew, to ask his forgiveness, but the Rabbi did not even let them come near him. He said: "May death be his punishment!" A few days later, the man died.

After the death of their leader, his associates came to Rabbi Loew and confessed their wicked deed; they defended themselves, however, by saying that the man who had just died, had persuaded them to do it. Rabbi Loew punished them by imposing a fine on them for the benefit of the Talmud school; in addition, he commanded them to observe forty fasts every year and read 150 psalms every Sabbath all their lives long.

*

NOTE. — In Rabbi Loew's book *Netiwot Olam* (first published in Prague in 1596, then later in Nowy Dwohr in 1809), pp. 60—64, this case is discussed on a legal basis at great length, and the decisions of the Rabbinical authorities are published. This theme also appears in his *"Predigt an Bussesabbattage"* (Sermon on Sabbath-day Atonement), 1583. The incident is further mentioned in the notes of Rabbi Solomon Loria's *Yam schet Schlomo*, written in the 16th century, to Talmud Babli tractate Baba Kama, chapter 8, paragraph 54, (as a reply to Rabbi Loew, without mentioning his name), in these words: "In reference to the family, about whom the report has spread that a brother had married his own sister in ignorance of the relationship, which was later discovered through the wart from birth..., many great men of the generation have become related to that very large family... and whoever will call this family by the name of 'Nadler', will deserve the same punishment as if he had called them 'bastard', namely, flogging, after which they will have to ask forgiveness." Compare this also to Talmud Babli Kiddushin; chapter 4, paragraph 4. Lastly, it appears from the book *Sera Berach*, notes to e tractate Berachoth by Rabbi R. Brachja Berach (first published in Halle in 1714), that in the 17th century this family was still one of the most distinguished, and the man who disgraced them, was severly punished by the Rabbinate.

PURIM JOY AND TRAGEDY

YEARS passed during which no blood accusation was raised against the Jews of Prague. But in the year 5349 (1589) trouble did break out again.

In Prague lived a rich and learned Jew by the name of Reb Aron Gins, who owned a leather-goods factory in a suburb, in which he employed a large number of Christian workmen. Among these were three brothers who lived with an old widowed mother, in a village not far from Prague. Two of the brothers were called Karl and Heinrich Kozlovsky respectively, while the third was called only by the nick-name Kozulek. This young man whom his mother, Jadwiga, called Johann, came into Reb Aron's employ as a fifteen year old lad. He developed into something of a rapscallion and Reb Aron was dissatisfied and would have liked to discharge him but for the fact that he was very efficient and diligent. Once, in the course of a quarrel with a fellow workman, Johann fell into a ditch and was injured in such a way that he was no longer able to work, and Reb Aron discharged him. Johann's brothers protested against this and it was finally agreed that Johann be taken back into service at half his former wages. As he was unable to work in the factory, Reb Aron took him as a house servant.

On Purim, as is the custom among Jews, Reb Aron gave a feast to his many friends and relatives. There was much jollity, and wine was freely imbibed according to the traditional rule. With great glee and spirit the company sang the beautiful melody *Shoschanot Yaakov*. Kozulek, who waited on the company, was more generously tipped than usual, this day being a special gift-giving festival. It was not until after midnight that the guests departed, leaving the host and the members of his household, who soon retired and, having consumed much wine in honor of the feast, fell fast asleep.

Kozulek Steals.

Kozulek thought this a good opportunity to enrich himself. He took the silver dining and drinking service as well as the silver time-piece of Reb Aron, and hurried home.

When, on the following morning, the theft and desertion were discovered, Reb Aron called for the Kozlovsky brothers and did not conceal from them his suspicion that they knew something of the whereabouts of their brothers and that they even had had a hand in his game. They hotly resented his suspicions and declared in the most positive manner that they had the slightest knowledge of the theft. Nevertheless, Reb Aron reported the matter to the authorities who searched the house of the Kozlovskys but without finding any trace of the pilfered articles. This increased the hatred of the two men against Reb Aron and they began to nurse a grudge and a desire for revenge.

The following Monday, the brothers came to work in the afternoon. Their lateness irritated Reb Aron who insinuated that it was probably due to a drunken debauch paid for with the stolen articles. But the Kozlovskys held their peace though their hearts were filled with resentment and anger.

On the next day, the two brothers spread the

report that Kozulek had disappeared without
leaving a trace and that the Jews must have
slaughtered him in preparation for their Passover. As this festival was but a few days off
this libelous report found ready credence and
spread like lightning through Prague and its
environs. Popular clamor influenced the authorities to institute an investigation in the course
of which some Christians came forward and told
how, one night as they were driving past the
Jewish cemetery, they came upon two men who
were digging a grave just outside of the wall.
They inquired of these men what they were about
and were told in a mixture of German and Yid-
dish that they were Jewish grave diggers and
that they had been ordered to bury a good-for-
nothing imbecile, who was neither Jew nor
Christian, in a grave outside the wall as the fellow was unfit to lie in consecrated ground.

The Corpse Exhumed.

Rabbi Loew and the communal officials were
next examined, but stoutly denied that any such
person had died or that they ever gave such
instructions to anybody. The Jewish grave dig-

176

gers also positively denied having received such orders.

Thereupon the authorities took the Christian witnesses to the cemetery and asked them to point out the scene of their encounter. A great crowd, including of course the two Kozlovskys, went along. Traces of a newly-made grave were found, and when it was opened the spectators were horrified to see taken from it the corpse of Kozulek, wrapped in a blood-stained sheet. The Kozlovskys ran forward, fell on their knees, crossed themselves and cried: "Brother! Brother!" Then turning to the crowd, they exclaimed: "Come, brothers, and sisters! Look! See how that cursed Jew, Aron Gins, has slaughtered our brother! It must have happened on that Purim night! He stupefied him with wine and when he fell asleep they killed him. That is why they all assembled at Aron's house that night! Now you know why the cursed Jew spread the libel that our brother had robbed him and fled! It was only to cover up his horrible crime!"

The crowd became threatening and a riot would have broken out on the spot, had not Rabbi Loew admonished the authorities that they would be held responsible for any disorders, pending the thorough sifting of the matter. The Kozlovskys now demanded that the police make a search of Reb Aron's house for any evidence which might connect him with the crime.

Although the authorities were suspicious from the outset that the whole affair had the earmarks of a criminal plot yet they could not refuse this demand, and the prefect of police, accompanied by a squad of soldiers and civillan court attendants, repaired to Aron's house and searched it thoroughly. Their efforts were fruitless until they came into the cellar. There, they came upon some clothes, which were soon identified as those of the dead Kozulek. There was nothing to be done but to arrest Reb Aron and close and seal his house until the matter had been cleared up.

The next day Reb Aron's house was the centre of morbid curiosity. Monks headed by an abbot took charge of the corpse of Kozulek to prepare it for Christian burial. Fiery speeches against the Jews were delivered.

The Jews of Prague were seized with terror and were afraid to appear upon the streets. Even Rabbi Loew was frightened. He was convinced of Reb Aron's innocence, but he had no ground on which to contradict the charge against him. The fiendish plot had been carried out with great cunning and it seemed that for once a lie was to triumph.

For a time, Rabbi Loew took no steps to save Reb Aron and his unhappy family. The only thing he did was to order the entire congregation to meet every day at dawn in the synagogues and to recite special prayers. It being the month of Nisan, no fast days were appointed.

Lives Endangered.

But when the priests issued an order forbidding Christians to trade with Jews and the entire economic life of the latter was in danger of extinction, Rabbi Loew changed his attitude. He adressed in a dream a question "above," asking how he could prove the innocence of the Jews and he received this answer: "Thou shalt thoroughly look and search and inquire; then will the sons turn on their tracks." Rabbi Loew was jubilant at this answer, reported it to his associates and encouraged them to have faith that God would soon bring the truth to light.

The day of the trial came, however, before anything had been discovered to prove Reb Aron's innocence, and the poor man was sentenced to fifteen years imprisonment, while his wife and three daughters were sentenced to six years each. This outcome threw the entire Jewish community into mourning.

It was only after the feelings of both Jews and Christians had cooled somewhat, that Rabbi Loew set diligently to work to establish Reb Aron's innocence. There were those who declared there had been a gross miscarriage of justice and on every hand there was evidence of divided opinion as to the guilt of the unfortunate Reb Aron.

Rabbi Loew sent two messengers secretly to the village in which the Kozlovsky brothers lived, to find out all they could about the two men and their mother. When the messengers returned without any information of value, Rabbi Loew concluded that there was only one way to learn the truth. "I must utilize supernatural agencies," he said. "The soul of a human being hovers over his grave for a whole year, for it is still related to its body during that time."

Golem Despatched.

Receiving permission from the authorities, he sent the Golem and a confidential assistant to investigate recent burials in the cemetery of the village in which the Kozlovskys lived. Accompanied by two police officers, Rabbi Loew's agents went to the village, and summoning the official grave diggers, repaired to the cemetery.

What Rabbi Loew expected happened. As the Golem examined the graves made within the preceding four months, he suddenly came to a stop on one of them, indicating by gesticulations that it was empty. The police officers at once sent a messenger to Prague to inform the prefect and Rabbi Loew. Both came, the prefect accompanied by several assistants, and Rabbi Loew by the most prominent members of his congregation. The grave was opened, and the fact established that it contained an empty coffin.

The police then called upon the parish priest in order to ascertain from the register who had been buried in this grave. The priest looked up his records and recalled that about three weeks before the Jewish Passover, he had given a permit for the burial of Johann, son of Judwiga Kozlovsky, to two men who claimed to be the dead man's brothers. The priest recalled, further, that the two men had explained that they had no money to pay for the burial and had tendered in lieu of payment a silver watch, which they said had been left to them by their deceased father. They had also asked that the funeral be private because Johann was an illegitimate child. The watch was easily identified as the property of Reb Aron, as it answered in every detail the description given by him to the police

The prefect then cross-examined Jadwiga, the mother. She at first pretended to know nothing, but her memory was quickly refreshed by a box on the ear, and she made the following deposition:

When, on the Saturday following Purim, the two brothers came home for the week-end, they found Johann on his death-bed. He had caught cold on the night of his escapade and as he was at best in poor health he sank rapidly and soon breathed his last. They then arranged with the priest for the burial, which was done with the help of an old grave-digger. A few days later they came at night to the cemetery, disinterred

182

the body, and buried it outside the wall of the Jewish cemetery of Prague. It was they who told some Christian travelers, passing by in a carriage, that they were burying a Jewish imbecile, who was not worthy of being buried in the cemetery proper. They had also made a bundle of the dead boy's clothing and thrown it into Reb Aron's cellar.

The mother also told where the other articles stolen from Reb Aron had been pawned, and she and the receiver of these were arrested and taken to Prague.

The two brothers, in the meantime, having got wind of the fact that their plot had been discovered, had left Prague.

Reb Aron, his wife and daughters were, of course, quickly released, completely cleared of all suspicion.

This episode attracted extraordinary attention in Prague and in the entire country, and increased the great respect in which Rabbi Loew was held.

THE AUDIENCE WITH THE KAISER

RABBI Loew submitted to Kaiser Rudolf II a memorandum enclosing therewith reports in full of all the ritual-murder trials that had taken place for the past ten years. He asked for an audience, for he had to lay before the Kaiser an urgent request in behalf of his coreligionists.

Although he had been brought up by Jesuits, in the country of ever-smoking funeral pyres, the Kaiser was nevertheless not without feeling of justice towards the Jews, so he granted the request in a most gracious manner.

One day, the Jews of Prague saw with astonishment a royal equipage drive through the portals of the Ghetto. Two courtiers handed Rabbi Loew a card entitling him to an audience, a most unusual distinction, and Rabbi Loew drove with them to the royal palace.

About three hours later, he returned home in a royal carriage, escorted by still higher court officials.

Rabbi Loew was in high spirits, and said to his confidential friends who were awaiting him anxiously: "I thank the Lord, praised be His name, that I have succeeded in removing from this earth the wrong of blood-accusations. The Kaiser spoke to me about a half hour and gave me his royal word that from now on he would not only root out blood-accusations in his country, but would also treat the Jews the same as the other subjects of his Kingdom, and would protect their rights." Outside of that no one knew what the Kaiser spoke to him about.

About ten days after this audience, a decree was issued by the Kaiser stating that no Jew in the future may be accused of ritual murder, for the Kaiser was fully satisfied that such accusation was false, that the Jews did not need any blood for religious ceremonies, and that the use of blood was a grave offence against the Jewish religion. Should a Christian raise any accusation against a Jew, the charge should be directed only against the individual that was guilty of the act, but not against the Jews in general. Moreover, the fact must be established by four incontestable witnesses. The Rabbi and the community representatives must be present at the judicial proceedings.

The contemporaries said then referring to Rabbi Loew:

"Seest thou a man diligent in his business? He shall stand before Kings!" (Prov. xxii, 29).

●

NOTE. — In the Hebrew paper „Hamagid" in Lyck, edited by Dr. L. Silbermann, there is published in issue No. 4 of the year 1872, a report in manuscript by Rabbi Jizchak Cohen, Rabbi Loew's son-in-law. The report reads:

„This day, Sunday, the tenth day of Adar of the year of 5352 after the creation of the world, an order was issued by Kaiser Rudolf II and directed through Prince Bertier to Mordecai Meisel and Jizchak Weisel, that my father-in-law Rabbi Loew appear in the castle, nay, in the apartment of the Prince. In accordance with this order he betook himself to the palace, accompanied by his brother Rabbi Sinaj and myself. When we arrived there, an attendant of the Prince showed us directly into a salon, which communicated with several other rooms; several passages also led from the Kaisers' palace to the Prince's palace. The Prince appeared shortly after our arrival; he greeted us with great cordiality, shook hands with each one of us, then escorted us to another chamber, where he himself invited us to be seated, nor did he let us bare our heads. After that, he led my father-in-law into another chamber, where he showed him to the most distinguished seat while he himself sat opposite facing him. The Prince conversed with him on confidential matters, but he spoke loud enough for us to hear him. There was a reason for their speaking loud, namely, that the Kaiser, who stood behind a curtain, might be able to hear the whole conversation. Then the curtain was drawn open quite suddenly, and the Kaiser stepped forth, addressed some questions to my father-in-law in connection with the conference, upon which he withdrew again behind the curtain. Then the Prince led my father-in-law back into the room where we sat, took leave of us with the most cordial bows, shook hands with us a second time and escorted us, all the way to the court-yard. The subject of the conference we must, however, keep a secret, as is customary in matters royal, but we hope, in due time, to be able to reveal it." In a postscript the writer adds: „This day, the 11th of Adar, the Prince informed the above mentioned Jizchak Weisel, that the Kaiser had had a conference with my father-in-law, and that he had found unusual grace in the eyes of the Kaiser. May the Almighty incline the hearts of the Kaiser and of his counsellors, favorably in behalf of the remnant of Israel, and may

187

He grant the Kaiser many years of happiness and blessing."

It is easy to presume that the above report refers to this audience, and if, as we suppose, the Rabbi Jizchak actually is the author of the source of my stories (see introduction), then he probably fulfilled his earlier promise through the above description of the audience.

THE GOLEM RUNS AMUCK

AS mentioned before, Rabbi Loew made it a custom, every Friday afternoon, to assign for the Golem a sort of programme, a plan for the day's work, for on the Sabbath he spoke to him only in extremely urgent cases. Generally, Rabbi Loew used to order him to do nothing else on Sabbath but be on guard and serve as a watcher.

One Friday afternoon, Rabbi Loew forgot to give him the order for the next day, and the Golem had nothing to do.

The day had barely drawn to a close and the people were getting ready for the ushering in of the Sabbath, when the Golem, like one mad, began running about in the Jewish section of the city, threatening to destroy everything. The want of employment made him awkward and wild. When the people saw this, they ran from him and cried: "Joseph Golem has gone mad!"

189

The people were greatly terrified, and a report of the panic soon reached the Altneu Synagogue where Rabbi Loew was praying.

The Sabbath had already been ushered in through the Song for the Sabbath day (Psalms xcii). What could be done? Rabbi Loew reflected on the evil consequences that might follow if the Golem should be running about thus uncontrolled. But to restore him to peace would be a profanation of the Sabbath.

In his confusion, he forgot that it was a question of danger to human life and that in such cases the law permits, nay, commands the profanation of the Sabbath in order that the people exposed to danger might be saved.

Rabbi Loew rushed out and, without seeing the Golem, called out into space: "Joseph, stop where you are!"

And the people saw the Golem at the place where he happened to find himself that moment, remain standing, like a post. In a single instant, he had overcome the violence of his fury.

Rabbi Loew was soon informed where the Golem stood, and he betook himself to him. He whispered into his ear: "Go home and to bed."

And the Golem obeyed him as willingly as a child.

Then Rabbi Loew went back to the House of Prayer and ordered that the Sabbath Song be repeated.

After that Friday, Rabbi Loew never again forgot to give the Golem orders for the Sabbath on a Friday afternoon.

To his confidential friends he said: "The Golem could have laid waste all Prague, if I had not calmed him down in time."

THE GOLEM IS DESTROYED

AFTER a long time had passed when the community was no longer molested by blood accusations, Rabbi Loew sent for his son-in-law, Rabbi Jizchak, the Priest, and his disciple, Jacob Sasson, the Levite—those who had participated in the creation of the Golem,—and he said to them: "Now the Golem has become superfluous, for a blood impeachment can by this time no longer occur in any country. This wrong needs no longer be feared. We will therefore destroy the Golem."

It was on *Lag-B'Omer* of the year 5353 (1593). Rabbi Loew ordered the Golem not to sleep that night in the Rabbinical house, but to take his bed over to the garret of the Altneu Synagogue and to sleep there. That was done in private, as it was about midnight.

When two o'clock came that night, there arrived at Rabbi Loew's house, his son-in-law

192

Rabbi Jizchak, the Priest, and his disciple, Jacob Sasson the Levite, and Rabbi Loew put the question to them as to whether a dead body, like the Golem, would constitute an object of impurity like unto any other dead body. [To touch the body of a dead person renders one unclean, according to Jewish law. See Numbers xix, 14.] The question was significant, because, if the answer were "yes," the Priest would not, have been able to participate in the act of destroying the Golem. [In the Bible, the Priest is forbidden to become unclean. Lev. xxi, 1.]

Rabbi Loew decided that this case was different, and that the Priest was able to participate in the destruction of the work.

They ascended to the garret of the Altneu Synagogue, the assistant, Abraham Chayim, walking in advance with two burning candles.

The three men began their work of destruction, the annihilation of the Golem.

Fundamentally, they did everthing in the reverse order to that followed in creating the Golem. If at the creation, they had stood at the feet of the Golem, opposite his head, they now stood at his head opposite his feet. Similarly, the words from the Book of Creation were read backwards. — After this task was accomplished, the Golem was transformed again into a clod of clay, what he was before life was instilled into him.

Rabbi Loew called the sexton Abraham Chayim, took the candles from him and ordered him to undress the Golem to his shirt.

He was then covered with old prayer robes and remains of Hebrew books, which, according to the Jewish custom, were stored in the garret of the synagogue.

Abraham Chayim burned the Golem's clothing, inconspicuously, following the order of Rabbi Loew.

In the morning, news spread in the Jewish ghetto that Joseph Golem had disappeared from the town during the night. Only a few individuals, "men of a higher station," knew the truth.

Rabbi Loew had it announced in all Synagogues and Houses of Prayer that it was strictly forbidden for anybody to mount to the garret of the Altneu Synagogue. Furthermore, the remains of torn prayer books and other sacred things were no longer to be stored there.

WHERE LIE THE REMAINS
OF THE GOLEM?

THE following legend was, until now, almost unknown. According to it, the remains of the Golem do not lie, as is popularly believed, in the garret of the Altneu Synagogue, but on the gallows-hill outside the city. The legend upon which this conclusion is based is as follows:

The sexton, Abraham Chayim, had long been going about with the idea of imitating Rabbi Loew and making a Golem of his own. He had been present on the bank of the Moldau River when the Rabbi had made the Golem and had taken note of the *Schem* (Name) which had given the Golem the breath of life. He too would, by the use of this Name, create such a man. His son-in-law, Ascher Balbierer, who spent much time poring over the Kabbala could, if need be, help in the execution of the plan. Now that the Golem lay lifeless, the will to awaken him and

195

put him to uses of his own surged up strongly in the breast of Abraham Chayim.

One night he was on the point of mounting to the garret in order to look upon the Golem. But he was terrified and his heart became weak. He initiated his brother-in-law, Abraham ben Secharja, the sexton of the Pinkas Synagogue, into the secret. On the following night both men climbed up to the garret of the Altneu Synagogue, took hold of the lump of clay which had at one time been the Golem, and carried it over to the nearby Pinkas Synagogue where they concealed it behind the *Almemor* (reading desk). To Ascher Balbierer, the son-in-law of Abraham Chayim, was assigned the task of finding out the *Schem* with the help of which the Golem could be called to life. When Ascher after sereval days stated that he believed that he had come upon the mystic alphabetical formula in the *Sepher Jezirah* (the book of creation), the three men carried the Golem, in the dead of night, from the synagogue in the Pinkas Gasse through various solitary streets and alleys, into the cellar of a house in the Zeikerl, also known as Zigeuner Gasse, which partly belonged to Ascher and in

196

which he lived. Down in the cellar, they tried one night after another to follow the process of Rabbi Loew and his disciples, according to the remembrance of Abraham Chayim. But these attempts were all absolutely without result.

At about this time, there broke out in Prague an epidemic in the course of which twelve hundred persons died. Two of the five children of Ascher Balbierer were also snatched away, although there was no case of the plague in any other house in that street. The wife of Ascher had from the beginning strenuously resisted the bringing of the Golem into her house because she feared that in case the action were discovered, her father would lose his position as sexton in the Altneu Synagogue, while her husband and her uncle would be punished for violating the command of the rabbinical council against anyone going up to the garret in which the remains of the Golem had been placed. Besides that, she noticed with considerable concern that, because of his nocturnal exertions, her husband had neglected his business. Now that the children were stricken, she cried that the misfortune had visited them because the Golem had been brought to the house, and when the children died her protestations could not be resisted.

After the two corpses had been washed and placed in their coffins, one of them was taken out of his and placed together with the other. The remains of the Golem were then placed in the empty coffin. A waggon was hired and the coffins were taken at nightfall to the cemetery for victims of the plague, outside of the city. Here Abraham Chayim and Abraham Secharja took the coffin with the Golem in it and carried it up to the Gallows Hill which lies one mile and two hundred yards from the Neistaedter Gate on the Vienna state road, and placed it on that side of the hill which is turned toward the city. That was on the evening of the 5th of Adar.

RABBI LOEW'S UTTERANCES ON THE GOLEM

AT the creation of the Golem two spirits were crowding one another that he (Rabbi Loew) might put life into the Golem through them: the spirit of the demon Joseph and that of the demon Jonathan. The spirit of the former was chosen, because it had already in the time of the Talmudic sages rendered service to the Jews in days of affliction. Besides, Jonathan was a being that could not keep any secrets.

* * *

Just as the spirit of the demon Joseph migrated into the Golem, and through him found *Tikun*, (resuscitation) so will all the spirits of the "Jew-demons" mentioned in the book Zohar, go through several migrations and will finally attain resuscitation, during which time they will render aid to the Jews in their exile in times of oppression, by means of supernatural miracles.

* * *

Legally, the Golem is exempt from the laws, both commands and prohibitions, even those which women and slaves are bound to observe.

* * *

There is no trace of good or bad instinct in the Golem, and all his actions are only like those of an automatic machine, that fulfills the will of its creator.

* * *

The Golem had to remain dumb, because, as an incomplete creation, he was unworthy that the *Neshamah,* the light of God, dwell within him. He was inhabited only by Nefesh (sensory being) and *Ruach* (spirit).

* * *

There could be lent to the Golem only a small portion of intelligence, *Daat* (knowledge). The other two intelligences, *Chochmah* (wisdom) and *Bina* (judgment), he could not be supplied with at all, because, as said above, there was no *Neshamah* dwelling in his being.

* * *

Even though the Golem did not reach the height *Neshamah,* still when Sabbath came, there was noticed on his face a change—it became illuminated. For does it not say in Zohar that on Sabbath the tension (*Schlitat ha-Dinim*) of the week-days ceases, for the Sabbath is the symbol of the light of the world, whose rays shed radiance in abundance over all the universe and pervade every being?

* * *

The Golem had to be created without any sex-instinct; for, if he had had that instinct, no woman would have been safe from him.

* * *

The Golem was never ill, for he was immune from every impulse to do evil.

* * *

Man is allowed to choose between his own impulses, the "good" and the "evil" [the words "thou shalt love God with all thy heart" the sages interpreted to mean "thou shalt love Him with both your impulses, the 'good' and the 'evil'."—Berachot 54a], and therefore cannot afford to perceive those hidden things that lie outside of palpable reality. But the Golem, who, as said above, had no impulse, could, like the animals and birds, demons and spirits, see all hidden things.   *   *   *

It is known that in the garden of Eden there are 24 varieties of odors, which contain all sorts of medicinal qualities. And those odors are the property-instincts of the various medicinal herbs and minerals. Every hour a different good odor emanates, which cleanses the world's atmosphere, and protects the human beings from inhaling harmful noxious air. For man to comprehend that moment of the emanation of the odors, were possible only if he were able to divest himself completely of every bodily property. If human beings were able to know how to comprehend that moment, there would be no sickness in the world. The Golem, who was created through the spirit, and with whom the body is only an outward cloak, perceived that moment. He caught the odors, and could not be overcome by any illness.

*   *   *

The Golem partakes of the everlastig belie; and will rise again at the end of all human existence, but in quite a different form.

*   *   *

The prohibition not to ascend to the garret of the Altneu Synagogue does not apply to the successor and the subsequent successors of Rabbi Loew to the Rabbinical seat. These may only look at the destroyed work, the Golem-image, but must not handle it in any way or attempt to bring it to life again.

* * *

The Golem could not be counted in a *Minyan*.

* * *

The Book Jezirah makes no direct mention in words of the creation of a Golem or of any other living being. Only from the letters one must be able to collect the hidden rays concealed in them, through which it is possible to give life to a lifeless body. But in order to be able to do that, one must be not only a learned man, but also a righteous man, a *Zadik*. The greatest master in the Book Jezirah was Bezalel, of whom it is said: that God filled him with the spirit of God, in wisdom, and in understanding and in knowledge and in all manner of workmanship (Exodus xxi, 2). With the aid of the book Jezirah, he was able to carry out all his holy duties in connection with building and adornment of the Tabernacle in the wilderness.

THE EXPULSION OF THE JEWS

IN the days of the great Rabbi Loew, it happened once that a King issued a command stating that all Jews must, under penalty of death and confiscation of property, leave the country within a set period of time. The Jews were greatly agitated, and, from far and wide, they came to Prague, to Rabbi Loew, who was considered among the Jews at the time as the Head of the Diaspora, in order that he might do something to avert the awful decree. When they arrived at Rabbi Loew's house, they found him in his room, striding back and forth slowly and majestically, while singing a sad, solemn, plaintive melody. As they approached him, he greeted them softly with the Jewish blessing of peace, and, without permitting them to speak, he said: "...and peace be with you on your departure, for the matter concerning which you have come to see me, will be all settled by tomorrow, God willing."

That night, the King had a dream. He dreamt

he was in his capital. It was a hot summer day, and he rode with his retinue to the outskirts of of the city to bathe in a flowing river at the foot of the forest. As he was a good swimmer, he swam across the whole width of the river, reached the bank on the opposite side, where, separated from his attendants, he wished to take a rest after his exertion, for a considerable length of time. All at once he saw, in deathly terror, that his men had gotten out of the water, had dressed themselves, and had driven away in their carriages. In vain he called to them, like one grown frantic, to wait for him, their King. He remained all naked and disconcerted, on the other side of the river, on the verge of unconsciousness. When he regained consciousness, it seemed to him best to seek his way home following the path in the forest.

In the forest he met several wood-cutters, to whom he revealed his identity. But the coarse men only made light of his appearance, and even let him feel their strength. He deemed himself happy when he succeeded in running away from them, and thus he roamed about in the forest, like a stray goat. He met an old beggar, who gave him the most necessary rags, and led him into the imperial street, where he encountered a number of people from his capital. He addressed them with words as follows: "I am your King, who has lost his way." But they turned their backs on him, in pity, and considered him as one whose mind was affected; for, had not the people seen the King, only a short while ago, in his capital, clad in royal attire?

Despairing of his fate, he wandered—so the King dreamt—from place to place, evading any revelation of his identity to any one. In his wanderings he reached Prague. By chance, he arrived at the ghetto, and he thought to himself: "The fate of this people, with their great past and their present low state, is the semblance of my own. This people, too, was great once, and yet, it is not recognized now."

He met an old Jew, whose patriarchal appearance inspired him with confidence, and he opened his heart to him. The old man showed himself at once obsequious, and said: "There is our Rabbi of superhuman wisdom, who knows how to interpret the riddle of riddles; he will give you counsel." The Jew led the King to Rabbi Loew, who received him as befits a King, and before even he heard him speak a word, he said: "A double of you has ascended your throne. He is here today and is riding to the Moldau to bathe there. When he will be in the water, arrange it so that you pay him back with the same coin." Rabbi Loew provided the proper clothes for him, cut his beard, grown unkempt, trimmed his nails and anointed his body with fragrant oils. After that, the King felt anew his former majesty.

Rabbi Loew said: "If you wish again to come to your power and regain your appearance, then sign this document in two copies, in which you will revoke the edict of the expulsion of the Jews." The King signed the document in duplicate.

Thus encouraged, he betook himself to the Moldau, found the company of people as Rabbi Loew predicted, and, when the false king and his attendants were in the water, he hastily clothed himself in the King's garments, and drove away... The King awoke from his dream.

The King staggered, when, upon looking around, he not only found on the table a copy of his order, with his own signature on it, but even the golden tray with the beard and the cuttings of nails...

Rabbi Loew had kept his word. The expulsion of the Jews did not take place.

*

NOTE. — A similar fate is said to have befallen King Solomon, of whom it is reported in the Talmud (Gittin, 37 a), that the King of demons, Ashmedai, (Asmodeus) assumed his countenance and ascended his throne.

SOLOMONIC WISDOM

THERE was a case in Prague, the issue of which aroused a great sensation. This was the story: In one large shop, separated by a wooden partition, there were two stores. One of them was occupied by a non-Jewish pork-butcher; the other was owned by a Jewish dealer in second-hand clothes, who sold old garments and all sorts of castoff articles. The partition had openings in it, so that one storekeeper could see distinctly what was going on in the store of the other. One day, the butcher noticed that the Jew was counting various coins. He at the same time took note what sum it made up, and thereupon went to the police, reported that such and such coins had been stolen from him and asked that the shopkeepers in the neighborhood be searched. Finally coins corresponding exactly with the report of the butcher were found in possession of the Jewish clothes-dealer, who was consequently arrested. The money was taken by the police as material evidence. The Jew protested his innocence, and explained that the butcher surely must have observed through an opening in the wall how he was counting the money; and was therefore able to give an exact count and description of it. Now, although the authorities believed that the clothing-dealer was innocent, because he was generally known as an honest man, while the pork-dealer's reputation on the contrary, was not good, it was not their function to decide these matters. It was customary, in such cases to apply to the Kaiser for a decision. When the incident was related to the Kaiser, he, too, could not pronounce any judgment. He sent for Rabbi Loew and asked his advice.

Rabbi Loew said:

"It is evident that the coins which a pork-butcher takes into his hands, must have fat on them. We will therefore attempt to throw the coins into a kettle of boiling water; if fat will come to the surface, it will be proof that the clothing dealer is guilty; otherwise, the butcher is making a false accusation."

210

The suggestion pleased the Kaiser immensely. The test was undertaken, and it was proved that the water remained quite clean. Then a number of coins were taken from the butcher's strong-box and placed in boiling water. Fatty globules came up to the surface of the water.

The Kaiser decided therefrom that the money rightly belonged to the clothing-dealer, and the butcher was fittingly punished.

KAISER RUDOLF IN CAPTIVITY

IT was in the month of Elul of the year 5353 (1593), when Rabbi Loew was suddenly summoned before Kaiser Rudolf; it was on a matter of extraordinarily great import, said the Kaiser's messenger.

The Kaiser received him, as usual, very cordially, but appeared to be very sad this time.

Rabbi Loew said: "Lord and Kaiser, what makes your Majesty so sad?"

The Kaiser replied: "I must tell you this in confidence: My ministers have submitted to me this day a bill for me to sign, which is extremely unfavorable for the Jews. I feel grieved for your people; hence my sadness, and therefore have I sent for you."

Rabbi Loew asked: "Could you not have simply refused to sign it, and then your grief would have ended?"

"This cannot be done as easily as you imagine, Rabbi," replied the Kaiser. "I have already given my chancellor my royal word that I will sign the bill; I cannot revoke it. Look, Rabbi, there in the drawer are the papers; I shudder to think of touching them, but I must, I am the Kaiser; I must not be influenced by sentiment..."

Rabbi Loew urged the Kaiser to destroy the papers. He, Rabbi Loew, could be bold enough to do it, for was not the Kaiser his friend? He urged Rudolf to do so again and again, but in vain. The Rabbi's words, however, made a deep impression on the Kaiser, and he became even more dejected. Finally, he said: "Accompany me to my pleasure-garden."

When they were in the garden, the Kaiser invited Rabbi Loew to sit by his side. And there they talked on sundry matters. Rabbi Loew avoided touching even with one more word upon the subject of the Jews, so as not to cause the Kaiser to grow still more sad.

Suddenly the Kaiser said: "I am feeling quite weary, and would like to sleep a while; please sit by me, and stay here till I wake again."

The Kaiser fell Asleep.

And there he had a dream, a wondrous dream.

One of his feudal princes, who reigned over a small state far away, sent word to the Kaiser, through a messenger, that from now on he did not consider himself as under his, the Kaiser's, sovereignty and consequently, he regarded himself released from all former obligations. The Kaiser became very angry thereat. He called at once a privy Council, and it was decided to declare war without delay against the rebellious Prince. The Kaiser himself headed his troops, and his intention was to dethrone the Prince. But already in the first battle, the Prince, who was commanding his army in person, was able to inflict defeat upon the Kaiser's troops. The main body of soldiers fell like heroes; the rest, together with their commanders, were taken into captivity. The Kaiser himself was not spared this fate. Thereupon he was brought to the Prince's capital and was imprisoned in a dungeon. During the day, he would stand at the little window in his cell and look out, his mind almost a blank. Through the same window was handed him his food: bread and water. Eleven years went by.

214

One day he espied, through the little window, his friend Rabbi Loew. He shouted with all his might: "O Rabbi Loew, save me!" Rabbi Loew approached the little window, extended his hand to him and said: "If I should free your Majesty from this situation, will your Majesty destroy the papers that contain unfavorable laws against the Jews?"

The Kaiser laughed bitterly and replied: "Is that you, the wise Rabbi Loew? What question are you asking me? Have I not been in captivity eleven years? Doubtless there is someone else on the throne." But Rabbi Loew insisted. "Let but your Majesty give me the key to the drawer; I wish to see whether the papers are still there; if they are, I will destroy them."

In his sleep, the Kaiser took the key out of his pocket and handed it to Rabbi Loew, who betook himself then to the Kaiser's cabinet, took the papers out of the drawer, and, after destroying them, went back to the pleasure-garden, where he found the Kaiser still asleep. He gave him back the key, and the Kaiser put it in his pocket.

And the Kaiser dreamt on: Rabbi Loew pulled

him out through the little window, led him back to his royal castle in Hradschin and seated him on the throne.

The Kaiser woke up, exultant with joy. And upon seeing Rabbi Loew by him, he embraced him and said:

"I thank you, Rabbi, that you have set me free from my bitter captivity. I see only now what a good friend I have in you." The Kaiser did not sign the bill against the Jews, but Rabbi Loew became since that day even more destinguished. All his life the Kaiser was convinced that Rabbi Loew had saved him from captivity.

Rabbi Loew recorded this event in a secret book. Only after his death—the Kaiser, too, had already departed—was the secret book discovered. Rabbi Loew states there that he had conjured up the Angel of Dreams.

And from that book were taken all these stories written here, in order that the future generations might know that God does not desert His people, Israel, and that, just when their misery is at its worst, help is at hand.

THE SUNKEN WALL

ONE day Kaiser Rudolf, induced to do so by a Minister, who was an enemy to Rabbi Loew, requested the latter to show him the Patriarchs and Fathers of the Tribes.

Rabbi Loew agreed to do so, only making one condition, which was, that the Kaiser should not laugh whatever he night see. The time and place for the incantation were fixed. In a lonely hall of the Hradschin Castle the mystic rites were performed. The Patriarchs and the Fathers of the Tribes appeared one after the other, in their own figures and the Emperor wondered at the size and strength of these men of ancient times. Each of the Tribal-fathers showed himself in a manner befitting his real nature. But when swift-footed Naphtali hovered over standing ears of corn and flax-stems the Emperor could not restrain himself any longer and laughed aloud. In an instant the apparition had disappeared and the vaulted ceiling sank in. The Kaiser would have been buried under it if Rabbi Loew had not forbidden the ceiling to sink further by uttering the SHEM (Name of God). To the present day the sunken vaulting in the hall, which has never been opened since, may be seen.

THE WONDERFUL PALACE

AT Kaiser Rudolf's court there was a
Minister, who envied the exalted Rabbi
Loew for the regard in which the Emperor held him and who became therefore his
enemy. He continually and on every occasion
slandered and accused him to the Emperor, who
however took no notice of the Minister's words
and grew more and more fond of Rabbi Loew
from day to day.

Now one day the envious Minister appeared
before the Kaiser and said:

"All your Ministers and Counsellors have
arranged festival-dances in your honour, only
your Jewish Privy-Counsellor, Rabbi Loew, on
whom you bestow your greatest confidence, has
not till now considered it his duty to pay homage
or show his allegiance to you by giving a festival.
I propose therefore that you should make trial
of his loyalty by commanding him to arrange a

feast in your honour within a short time. The
wicked man thought in his heart that the Rabbi,
being poor, would not be able to arrange a banquet and would therefore lose the Kaiser's
favour."

Next day the Kaiser said to Rabbi Loew:
"I feel a desire that you should arrange a ban-
quet in my honour as all my Counsellors and
Ministers have already done! You are my Privy-
Counsellor, you know!"

"It will be as you, my Master and Kaiser
desire," answered Rabbi Loew, "but you must
give me a space of four weeks that I may prepare everything and I will arrange a banquet
which will surpass in splendour all those which
have been given in your honour until now."

The Emperor replied: "The space of time shall
be granted you, but take care that the banquet
be indeed a fine one, in order that your enemies
may not be able to take their revenge on you."

When the Kaiser fold the Minister what
Rabbi Loew had promised, he laughed and said:
"How can he prepare such a splendid feast? He
is a poor man. He was mocking you with false
promises."

220

"You will see," said the Kaiser, "that he will keep his word for he has never told a lie."

But the Minister did not believe it and said: "You will see he will be proved a liar."

Day for day he sent a messenger to Rabbi Loew's house in order to find out if he were preparing the banquet. But ever the messenger came again and reported that the Rabbi Loew was seated at his table quite absorbed in his great books. Even on the day on which the feast was to take place he found Rabbi Loew deep in his studies. The Minister was overjoyed.

An hour before the banquet was to begin Rabbi Loew came to the Kaiser and begged that he would come with all his Ministers and Counsellors to the banquet. The Kaiser, who was convinced of the godliness of Rabbi Loew, went with all his suite, including of course the envious Minister, to the Rabbi's house. They came to his modest dwelling and found him poring over a book. The Minister, rejoicing at the sight, looked into the Emperor's face as if he would say: "Well who is right?"

Rabbi Loew rose and said: "Now let us go to the feast!" He led his high guests to the river

Moldau. There stood a glorious palace! He invited his guests to enter and all were astonished at the splendour which reigned there. The table was laid and many servants stood ready. The Kaiser spoke not a word but seated himself at table; so did the Ministers. The appointments of the table were of gold, studded with precious stones, while the most costly and exquisite fruit were piled upon the beautiful dishes, as is the custom in Rulers' houses.

"Enjoy all to your hearts' content," said Rabbi Loew, "only be careful to take nothing away with you."

After the meal was over Rabbi Loew invited his guests to follow him into a lovely pleasure-garden, in which beautiful fruit-trees grew. Then the exalted guests took their leave of Rabbi Loew and prepared to leave the palace. To their surprise they saw the Minister, who was the Rabbi's enemy, sitting in his place unable to move. The Kaiser, being informed of the fact, re-entered the palace and locking at the Minister with pity said: "Beg the Rabbi and he will free you, for it surely was his will that this should happen to you."

Then the Minister spoke in a sorrowful voice and said: "I beg the Rabbi to set me free."

The Rabbi turned to the Kaiser saying: "I warned the company not to take anything away; but he has stolen a cup and for that reason he is not able to move. The Minister then confessed with shame that he had really taken a cup and handed it to Rabbi Loew after which he was able to rise from his seat. Then the Kaiser begged Rabbi Loew to lend him the cup that he might have one made like it and added: "Perhaps it is possible that I may buy it?" Rabbi Loew answered: "I cannot sell it, for it is only lent to me, but keep it till it is claimed."

The Kaiser took it joyfully. Ohn the way home he said to the Minister: "Now have I convinced you that Rabbi Loew is my best friend and that your assertion that he is not loyal is false? I dismiss you and never let me see your face again."

Of course the Kaiser and his Counsellors were much puzzled as to how Rabbi Loew came by the wonderful palace. But some weeks afterwards they learned the secret.

In a far-off land a King had arranged a great

feast to which many Kings and Princes were invited. He had a palace built for this occasion and
furnished it with all sorts of treasures and costly
things. But one day the palace disappeared with
all its appointments, even including the servants.
Nobody could understand how it had happened.
But in a few days the palace reappeared in its
proper place. Only the costly meals and the
exquisite beverages were wanting and one costly
cup over the loss of which the King grieved. He
sent word to all his ambassadors in the different
countries where they were stationed ordering
them that they should endeavour to find out all
they could about the mysterious event and if
possible, to trace the cup.

When the Kaiser heard of this he immediately informed Rabbi Loew who commanded that
the cup be sent back without delay.

The Kaiser gave the messenger a letter to
the King, written by himself, in which he informed the latter of the wisdom of one of his
Privy-Counsellors.

THE BANQUET

MANY of the most distinguished men of that time had gathered round Kaiser Rudolf, such as Tycho de Brahe, Johannes Keppler and others. The Kaiser's great learning, as well as the favour he showed to men of science, had not only attracted many alchemists and astrologists from far-off lands, but had induced many nobles to take up the pursuit of knowledge themselves.

On his estate, near Prague, there lived a rich and powerful Count, who was much devoted to Alchemy and Astrology. Having heard of the great learning of the exalted Rabbi Loew, he hastened to make his acquaintance and often invited him to his castle. Rabbi Loew, on his side, was pleased to have intercourse with a nobleman so versed in learning, and the scientific arguments, which were so often held between them, stimulated the exalted Rabbi to further and deeper researches. One day the Count paid a visit to Rabbi Loew in his own house. He found him surrounded by four hundred of his followers and expressed his astonishment that it should be possible to take so large a number of scholars into so small a house.

Rabbi Loew laughed and said: "I should have room enough for a threefold number."

"That is incredible," answered the Count.

Thereupon the Rabbi: "I will prove it to you on some occasion!"

Visiting the Count again a few days later, he said to him: "Please do me the favour of taking part at a banquet with all your friends" The Count accepted the invitation, appointed the day, promising to come with many of his friends.

On the appointed day the Count and a great company of his friends appeared before Rabbi Loew's modest dwelling. The latter hastened out and led his distinguished guests into the interior of the little house. The Count was amazed, for so modest as the house appeared to be from the outside, so splendid and so wonderful was it on the inside. Wherever he gazed he perceived that it was built according to the highest laws of architecture. The broad staircase was laid with the richest carpets and the walls were covered with paintings, the artistic conception and portrayal of which were truly delightful. The guests entered the ante-chamber, a long flight of appartments stretched beyond. Whatever Art could offer was placed to view in a most tasteful manner. The Count and his friends were quite astonished at the profound appreciation of Art shown by their host, Rabbi Loew. The time for the banquet having come, the double doors leading to the Dining-hall opened as at an order from above. There stood a long table spread with the most splendid appointments; golden cups, large silver dishes, savoury foods. The Count and his friends, who had often sat at the royal table, wondered at the immeasureable wealth here displayed and confessed to each other in a low tone that these table-appointments far surpassed those of the Emperor himself. During the course of the meal the Count secretly appropriated one of the golden salt-cellars.

The banquet ended, the guests left the dwelling of Rabbi Loew with many protestations of their complete satisfaction.

A short time after the Count read one day the strangely surprising news, that, in a distant country, a castle had suddenly disappeared ; on the next day it had been found again in its proper place, intact with all its treasures excepting—one valuable salt-cellar! Then the Count remembered the salt-cellar he had taken with him.

THE „KABBALA"

WHEN, some days afterwards, Rabbi Loew visited the Count again the latter said to him: "I know that you are versed in the Kabbala and I desire that you instruct me in this mystery."

Rabbi Loew answered: "It is quite impossible for me to fulfil your desire; it is the peculiarity of this kind of knowledge that even a Jew seldom understands it rightly; all the more would a non-Jew be liable to misunderstandings."

The Count was angry and said in a commanding tone: "In spite of this I wish to fathom the Kabbala: and I command you to instruct me in the same."

Deeply moved Rabbi Loew answered: "Even a Jew has the greatest difficulties to overcome if he will devote himself to the study of the Kabbala and many a clear head has become confused thereby. Now consider, I beg you, how difficult of approach and dangerous it must be for a non-Jew."

"It is exactly this difficulty and danger," said the Count, "which makes me desire to understand it. No excuse will avail you to leave my wish unfulfilled."

"I cannot do it," was Rabbi Loew's answer.

The Count became enraged, "You dare refuse me?" he cried, "I will compel you to do it; I wish it! and you, Jew, have no right to say no. Do not raise my wrath! I am the Kaiser's friend, as you well know, and myself powerful; your life is at stake as well as the welfare of the Jews in our land, if you refuse to fulfil my wish." Quite frightened Rabbi Loew answered: "This compulsion makes it my duty to fulfil your desire. But you must grant me a delay; I must summon my comrade, Rabbi Abraham, from Saragossa, in Spain to come to Prague in order that he may help me to carry out this terribly difficult work."

"I grant you a delay of three months," said the Count, "see that you get your friend to Prague by that time so that you can then begin with the instruction."

The Rabbi hastened home, lost in thought. He

withdrew into his little room and pondered long as to what he should do in this unpleasant situation. Should he write to his comrade and fellow-scholar, Rabbi Abraham? What would he say when he learned that the reason of his summons to Prague is nothing more nor less than to open the gates of the Kabbala to a non-Jew. And how if he refuse? What terrible consequences would this call forth? Rabbi Loew prepared to put a "dream-question" and beg advice from Heaven. He fell asleep. Suddenly he was awakened by a strange man looking kindly into his face. Rabbi Loew could hardly believe his eyes when he recognized his friend, Rabbi Abraham.

"How did you get here," cried Rabbi Loew quite astonished, "did you know how much I need you? the welfare of the Jews in Prague is at stake!"

Rabbi Abraham answered: "You do not need to picture to me in what distress you are. I know what it is about and for that reason I am here. What you have experienced with the Count was revealed to me last night in a dream and I set out at once, for I knew that my presence would help you. The journey only lasted a few hours for I made use of a "SHEM" (Name of God) and shortened the way. And now, be at ease, I will instruct the Count."

Rabbi Loew sent word to the Count by his servant Chayim, that he would come on the following day with his friend, Rabbi Abraham, to begin the instruction: a secret room should be prepared, wrote Rabbi Loew.

On the following day the two learned men went to the Count's castle and Rabbi Loew introduced his friend as a fellow-scholar.

Rabbi Abraham bowed and said: "Forgive me, mighty Count, if I venture to prepare you by a few words for the instructions."

The Count answered: "Shall we not first descend into the room which I have had prepared in the subterranean vaults for this purpose."

They descended silently. The room which they entered had a peculiar aspect. It was hung with black cloth as if to show by the darkness which reigned that something mysterious should happen here. Only one lamp placed at the side shed its dim light over the scene. The three men who stood here opposite one another remained in silence. After a long time had elapsed Rabbi

Abraham spoke and said: "O Count before I begin to reveal the secrets of the holy Kabbala to you I must address a word of warning to you. Know then that the Kabbala is rooted in the pure belief in the *Highest* and that only those who are pure and holy are worthy to receive it. He, who freely and without fear wills to draw aside the veil of secrecy and gaze into the future must have a blameless past. I ask you therefore—is your conscience clear?"

The Count answered in a firm voice: "My conscience is clear!"

"Turn your gaze backwards", said the Rabbi Abraham, sternly, "look behind you."

The Count did so and started back with a despairing cry.

"Do you know them?" asked Rabbi Abraham.

"My God, my God, I know them! my sister and her child," murmured the Count.

"You, o Count, are guilty of the death of both of them," said Rabbi Abraham, "see how your sister with the child on her arms gazes out of the darkness!"

"O Lord have pity!" came brokenly from the lips of the Count.

The Count stood for some minutes as if turned to stone, then he said in a low tone: "You know my sin but you will be silent and not reveal my guilt. But in myself the misdeed cannot be silenced; it burms like fire in my veins." Then he said to Rabbi Loew: "I see now that I am unworthy to be instructed in the Holy Kabbala. I beg your pardon for pressing and threatening you so."

They ascended again and after a long conference the Count dismissed them assuring Rabbi Loew of his particular favour.

But from that day on he took care not even to mention the word KABBALA.

DEATH

IT was the custom of the great Rabbi Loew, evry night, when the hour of twelve struck, to recite the midnight lamentation. Then he would go, accompanied by his faithful attendant, Abraham Chayim, to the Altneu Synagogue opposite his abode. There he would speak with the souls of the dead, who, as is well know, assemble in the great synagogue after midnight. During this time, Abraham Chayim would remain in the vestibule. After an hour spent in this weird occupation, Rabbi Loew would return home and lay himself down to sleep for the few hours remaining before dawn.

On the night of the 11th of Elul, 5369, the same program was followed, but Rabbi Loew had scarcely fallen asleep after his visit to the synagogue, when he had a terrifying dream. He stood before a great court, the gate of which was open. As he went in, he was struck by a

horrifying picture. At an altar, stood a man of
unusually imposing presence, from whose eyes
came flashes as of lightning. In his hand he held
a bloody knife. A long line of young men whom
Rabbi Loew recognized as his pupils stood
awaiting slaughter. They all looked up to him,
their beloved master, so sorrowfully, that his
heart was pierced with pain and pity. The
terrible giant slew one youth after the other in
swift succession. Rabbi Loew saw the blood
flowing from the severed necks of the slaughtered
youths. Their blood dyed the earth a dark red.
Suddenly, he caught sight of his son-in-law,
Rabbi Yitzchak ben Simson the priest, and of
Jacob ben Chayim Sasson, the Levite, his favo-
rite, pupil. Both had assisted him at the creation,
and then, again, later, at the destruction of the
Golem. He saw the terrible man stretch out his
hand toward Yitzchak. At this Rabbi Loew
tore the knife from his hand and called out,
"Stop, thou angel of destruction! A truce to
these murders!"... He awoke.

Terrified, he sat up and looked about him.
It seemed to him that he still saw the blood and
he began to tremble in every limb for he

236

suspected that something was afoot which did not bode good. He sprang up like one who wishes to avert a great calamity, washed his hands, and began striding nervously up and down the room. He knew that, through the dream, he had been warned that his community was threatened by a misfortune and that he was called upon to prevent it.

Suddenly, his eye caught a light in the window of the Altneu Synagogue opposite. He stepped to his window and looked through the court, shrouded in darkness, into the interior of the synagogue. It was illuminated. What was going on there at this unearthly hour? Rabbi Loew mused for a while. Did this portend a new plot of the foes of Judaism? Only a short time before they had laid a vial of human blood in the Holy Ark. But the protection of God had saved the house of Israel from this threatening misfortune and had delivered the evil-doers over to justice.

The Rabbi went into the chamber of his servant, Abraham Chayim, and woke him. "Quick, take the keys and follow me!" he exclaimed. In a few moments both had donned their hats and coats and were running down the stairs. Rabbi

Loew ran as fast as he could to the synagogue, followed by Abraham Chayim. The Rabbi quickly unlocked the doors and both stepped into the vestibule. While Abraham Chayim remained here, Rabbi Loew strode into the interior.

His blood curdled in his veins at the sight which met his eyes. He saw the same man who had appeared in his dream standing at the *Almemor*. In his right hand was a bloody knife, while in his left he held a long scroll upon which were written various names in blood-red ink. The spectral figure moved his lips and called out the names one after the other. Rabbi Loew listened understandingly. They were the names of those whom the Unknown in his dream had slain. The last name he heard was his own,—it was at the foot of this list of death. Now Rabbi Loew understood that the was in the presence of the Angel of Death in all his fearsome form. He sprang up to him and with a sudden and violent motion, tore the scroll from his hand. The Angel of Death remained motionless,—towering and calm he stood there.

Rabbi Loew sprang to the doors. In the vestibule he found his servant trembling from head to

238

foot for he had heard the terrible one call out his name also. Like a victorious warrior carrying his booty, Rabbi Loew went to his house with the captured scroll pressed to his breast. There he read the names, and his heart was expanded with joy for he believed that he had saved the bearers of these names from death. Again and again he read the names of the saved. They included all the members of his congregation.

Suddenly he noticed that one corner of the scroll was torn away. This meant that a remnant of the paper upon which probably a name was written had remained in the hand of the Angel of Death. Whose name could it be? Rabbi Loew thought and thought but he could not guess, for the scroll which he had contained the names of all the members of his congregation; not one was missing.

A week passed. All his disciples were well and Rabbi Loew now was quite sure that he had put off their death. On the seventh day he held a feast of thanksgiving. He related to his followers the whole episode and they thanked Heaven for their good fortune. But soon after the feast Rabbi Loew caught a violent cold, and, on the 18th of Elul

5369, his noble soul departed from its earthly tenement. *On the piece of paper which had remained in the hand of the Angel of Death was his name.* The noble teacher in looking over the scroll for the missing name had entirely forgotten to look for his own. He whose name had been the last one on the sheet was the first to fall.

NOTES ON THE ILLUSTRATIONS

Altneu-Synagoge (Old-New School.) This old Synagogue, built in Byzantine style and probably almost a thousand years old, is still today one of the greatest sights of Prague and, with the one in Worms, the oldest Jewish House-of-God in Europe. Everyone looks with a certain awe at the old gloomy building with it's narrow windows, it's high gables and it's brick roof so worn by time and weather, which, as a monument of long past times and storms, reaches high above the tangle of narrow lanes about it.

Many of the tenderest legends are connected with this Synagogue. Some of the most beautiful shall be recorded here.

I. The Old-New School was built by a group of immigrants after the expulsion of the Jews from Palestine. The builders had taken stones with them from the destroyed Temple in Jerusalem, which they now introduced into the foundation walls of the newly-built Synagogue. They built this House-of-God "Al-Tenai", that is "with reservation" and made a vow that, when God should have redeemed Israel through the Messiah and led Her back into the Holy Land they would leave this, their new home, and take the Synagogue with them.

241

II. After the destruction of Jerusalem, Angels carried a part of Solomon's Temple to Prague, where a Jewish Community already existed. They revealed themselves to the Elders of the Jews in Prague and commanded them that the Synagogue should remain for ever just as they had brought it there, and that no-one should venture to repair it, for if he did so, he would surely die.

And so it happened that once, when the Elders had given a Masterbuilder the order tho repair the edifice, the builder and his assistants fell from the roof and they, as well as the Elders, died before the repairs were even commenced.

III. In Prague there stood a Synagogue, which had been built by the Jews on their arrival. When the building no longer met the needs of the Community, the Elders decided to errect a new one, larger and of stone, there, on the spot where a small hill rose. On demolishing and carrying away the old building, they came suddenly upon walls; yes, upon whole great walls built of mighty square blocks of stone. The further they dug, the more certainly they recognized the fact, that these walls belonged to an ancient Synagogue. And when they found a parchment scroll on which there was writing in Hebrew characters, they could doubt no longer. At that time there were two Jews in Prague. messengers from Jerusalem, who advised the Jews living there to build the Synagogue on the pattern of the one in Jerusalem; the windows to be so finished that they should not be broader on the outside than on the inside; to place the Holy of Holies on a lower level so that one must descend to it by a flight of steps, for it is written: "Out of the depth do I call upon Thee, O God," (Psalm 130).

IV. In the year 1558 a great fire broke out in the Jewish Quarter, during which everything fell a prey to the roaring flames; only the Old-New Synagogue stood untouched above the sea of fire. From all sides great thick black clouds of smoke rolled up and all was devastated, and ruined in the fierce blaze; only onto the Altar did no spark fly and no tile fell from the roof. Two white doves alighted on the dark old gable and remained there in spite of the suffocating smoke which could not drive them away. Then, suddenly, they rose on their white pinions and were lost to sight in the clouds.

The Old Jewish Cemetery in Prague. It lies in the so-called Josefstadt, the former Jewish quarter, there where, still some few years ago, little houses and crooked lanes presented a picture of a mediaeval Jewish town. Now there are broad streets and new houses there, while a great part of the Jewish Cemetery itself has fallen a victim to the new time. This cemetery is very old and was probably founded by the first of the Jewish settlers in Prague. According to a legend it already existed in the time of Libuscha, the legendary Bohemian Duchess, the foundress of Prague. Here, also, is the grave of Rabbi Loew. A large chiselled Vault marks his resting-place, covered by thousands of little stones. (It is an old custom to lay little stones on the graves of the "Great in Israel".) Thirty of his followers lie buried in a circle round their Master. Many other celebrated men of Jewry are bedded here for their last sleep, such as Mordechai Meisl, the greatest benefactor of his time and the founder of the Meisl-Synagogue existing to this day, and the celebrated Traveller, Physician and Mathematician Josef del Medigo de Candis, a scholar of Galileo Galilei.

Tyco de Brahe, the great Danish Astrologer, whom Kaiser Rudolf had called to Prague. His monument is to be found in the Teinkirche in Prague. Max Brod, the well known poet of Prague, gives a fine description of this character in his novel, "Tyco Brahe's Way to God". (Munich, Kurt Wolf.)

The picture given here is taken from an old engraving.